GUINEA PIG
CARE FOR BEGINNERS

The Complete Family Guide to Choosing, Caring For, and Understanding Your Pet

GUINEA PIG CARE FOR BEGINNERS: *The Complete Family Guide to Choosing, Caring For, and Understanding Your Pet*

Copyright © 2025 by Dylanna Press

All rights reserved. No part of this publication may be reproduced, distributed, or transmitted in any form or by any means, including photocopying, recording, or other electronic or mechanical methods, without the prior written permission of the publisher, except in the case of brief quotations embodied in critical reviews and certain other noncommercial uses permitted by copyright law.

Disclaimer: The information contained in this book is for educational purposes only and is not intended as a substitute for professional veterinary care. While every effort has been made to ensure the accuracy of the information presented, the author and publisher assume no responsibility for errors, omissions, or any outcomes related to the use of this information. Always consult with a qualified veterinarian for medical advice regarding your pet's health.

The advice and strategies contained herein may not be suitable for every situation. This work is sold with the understanding that the author and publisher are not engaged in rendering veterinary, medical, or other professional services. If professional assistance is required, the services of a competent professional should be sought.

ISBN: 978-1-64790-443-2
Publisher: Dylanna Press
First Edition: 2025
Printed in the United States of America
10 9 8 7 6 5 4 3 2 1

For information about special discounts for bulk purchases, please contact:

Dylanna Publishing, Inc.
www.dylannapublishing.com

Contents

Introduction: Your Guinea Pig Adventure Begins Here! 5

Chapter 1: Is a Guinea Pig Right for You? 10

Chapter 2: Why Two Is Better Than One 21

Chapter 3: Setting Up Your Guinea Pig's Dream Home 34

Chapter 4: Bringing Your Guinea Pigs Home 43

Chapter 5: Understanding Your Guinea Pig 51

Chapter 6: Feeding Your Guinea Pigs Right 59

Chapter 7: Handling and Bonding 77

Chapter 8: Grooming and Physical Care 84

Chapter 9: Keeping Your Guinea Pig Healthy 93

Chapter 10: Daily, Weekly, and Monthly Care 105

Chapter 11: When Challenges Arise 113

Chapter 12: Growing Together 123

Quick Reference & Emergency Guide 130

Index 132

Introduction: Your Guinea Pig Adventure Begins Here!

Are you thinking about getting a guinea pig? Maybe you've already fallen in love with one (or two!) at the pet store or animal shelter, or perhaps your family is trying to decide if guinea pigs would be the right pets for you. Either way, you've come to the right place!

This book is written especially for kids like you (ages 10 and up) and your parents who want to provide amazing care for guinea pigs. We know you're smart enough to handle real information about pet care, and we respect that you want to do things right from the very beginning.

Why This Book Is Different

Unlike other pet guides that talk down to kids or overwhelm families with complicated advice, this book treats you like the capable, caring person you are. We'll give you the honest truth about guinea pig ownership—both the wonderful parts and the challenging parts—so you can make great decisions and provide excellent care.

You'll learn everything you need to know to:

- Choose the right guinea pig breed and companions for your family
- Set up a habitat that makes your guinea pigs truly happy and healthy
- Develop daily care routines that work with your busy life
- Recognize and solve problems before they become serious
- Build strong, trusting relationships with your pets
- Handle the entire journey from adoption through your guinea pigs' senior years

What Makes Guinea Pigs Special Pets?

Have you ever heard a guinea pig "wheek" with excitement when they hear the refrigerator door open? Or watched one do a happy little jump called "popcorning" when they're feeling joyful? Guinea pigs aren't just adorable—they're incredibly social, communicative animals with amazing personalities.

Unlike many small pets, guinea pigs are **naturally social creatures** who love companionship. They talk to each other (and to you!) with a whole vocabulary of squeaks, purrs, and chutters. They're big enough to be **gentle lap pets**, yet small enough to manage easily. Most importantly, they give you something really special: the chance to watch intelligent, social animals interact and thrive in the loving home you create for them.

Guinea pigs are often called "cavies" (from their scientific name *Cavia porcellus*), and they've been beloved pets for hundreds of years. They're not related to pigs at all—they got their name from early traders who brought them from South America. These amazing animals have been bred into many beautiful varieties, each with their own care needs and personalities.

Every day with guinea pigs brings something to smile about. You might wake up to gentle squeaking as they hear you moving around, knowing that breakfast is coming. You'll discover that these animals have distinct personalities—some are brave explorers, others are gentle snugglers, and many are little comedians who find creative ways to make you laugh.

Unlike hamsters or other nocturnal pets, guinea pigs are most active during the same hours you are. This means you can enjoy their company after school, watch them play during weekend mornings, and even have them snuggle on your lap while you read or watch TV.

What Makes a Great Guinea Pig Owner?

Great guinea pig owners aren't born knowing everything—they're made through learning, practice, and genuine care for their pets. The best guinea pig families share a few important qualities:

They're committed learners who understand that good pet care requires knowledge and preparation, not just good intentions. Guinea pigs have specific needs that differ from other pets, and successful owners take time to understand these requirements.

They're realistic planners who think through the time, space, and money required for proper guinea pig care before bringing their pets home. This includes planning for pairs of guinea pigs, since these social animals do best with companions.

They're patient observers who take time to understand their individual guinea pigs' personalities, communication styles, and social dynamics. Each guinea pig is unique, and great owners learn to read their pets' signals and needs.

They're problem-solvers who stay calm during challenges and seek help when they need it. Guinea pig ownership brings learning opportunities, and the best families approach these as chances to grow rather than sources of stress.

They're in it for the long haul, understanding that guinea pigs can live 6-8 years and remain committed to excellent care throughout their pets' entire lives.

Does this sound like you and your family? If so, you're already on the path to becoming excellent guinea pig owners!

How to Use This Book

This book is designed to grow with you throughout your guinea pig ownership journey. You might read it cover-to-cover before getting your guinea pigs, or use it as a reference guide when questions arise. Either approach works perfectly!

Each chapter builds on the previous ones, but they're also designed to stand alone when you need specific information quickly.

A Note to Parents

While this book is written primarily for young readers, it's designed to be a valuable resource for the entire family. Children ages 10-13 can understand and implement most of the care information with appropriate adult supervision and support.

Remember that regardless of your child's enthusiasm and commitment, parents remain ultimately responsible for pet welfare. This book will help you understand what that responsibility entails while supporting your child's growth as a pet caregiver.

Guinea pigs require more complex care than some small pets due to their social needs, specific dietary requirements, and longer lifespans. This makes them excellent teaching pets for families ready for a meaningful commitment.

Your Journey Starts Now

Guinea pig ownership is an incredible opportunity to develop responsibility, learn about animal behavior, and experience the joy of caring for intelligent, social creatures. It's also a chance to create lasting family memories while discovering just how amazing these animals can be.

Whether this is your family's first pet experience or an addition to your existing pet household, approaching guinea pig care with knowledge, preparation, and genuine commitment sets you up for years of rewarding experiences. The social nature of guinea pigs means you'll likely be caring for at least two pets, which doubles the joy while teaching valuable lessons about animal relationships and social dynamics.

Are you ready to become the kind of guinea pig owner that every guinea pig deserves? Let's begin this amazing journey together!

Ready to start? Chapter 1 will help you determine if guinea pigs are truly right for your family, while giving you realistic expectations about what guinea pig ownership actually involves. We'll also explore the different breeds and help you understand which might be the best fit for your situation. Let's make sure you're prepared for success from day one!

Chapter 1: Is a Guinea Pig Right for You?

1.1 Meet the Amazing Guinea Pig

Have you ever watched a guinea pig "popcorn"—jumping straight up in the air with pure joy? Or heard one wheek so loudly when they hear the refrigerator door that you wonder how such a big sound comes from such a small animal? If you're reading this book, you've probably already fallen in love with these amazing creatures.

Guinea pigs aren't just cute pets—they're incredibly intelligent, social animals with complex personalities and fascinating communication abilities. Unlike many pets that sleep when you're awake, guinea pigs are most active during the same hours you are, ready to greet you after school with enthusiastic squeaking and charming antics.

FUN FACT
Guinea pigs can purr like cats when they're happy and relaxed!

What makes guinea pigs such special pets? They're the perfect size for comfortable holding and lap snuggling, they don't need walks like dogs, and they

Real Guinea Pig Success Stories

Lola (Age 11, Colorado): *"I was worried about getting two pets at once, but Cinnamon and Nutmeg have been perfect together. They teach each other things and comfort each other when one is scared. Watching them has taught me so much about friendship. Now when I see them snuggled up together, it makes me feel happy and proud that I'm giving them such a good life."*

The Thompson Family (Parents with 8, 10, and 13-year-old children): *"We wanted pets that would bring our family together while teaching responsibility. Our guinea pigs—Luna, Stella, and Comet—have exceeded our expectations. The kids learned to divide care tasks, work as a team during cage cleaning, and even developed a schedule for individual bonding time with each pig. It's amazing how these animals brought out the best in our children's teamwork skills."*

won't knock over your favorite things like cats might. But maybe most importantly, they give you something really unique: the chance to watch highly social animals interact with each other and with your family in ways that create lasting bonds and daily entertainment.

The Daily Wonder of Guinea Pig Life

Each day with guinea pigs brings moments of pure joy and discovery. You'll wake up to gentle morning greetings as they hear you moving around the house. Their excited wheeking when they hear the vegetable crisper drawer tells you they know exactly what time it is—salad time!

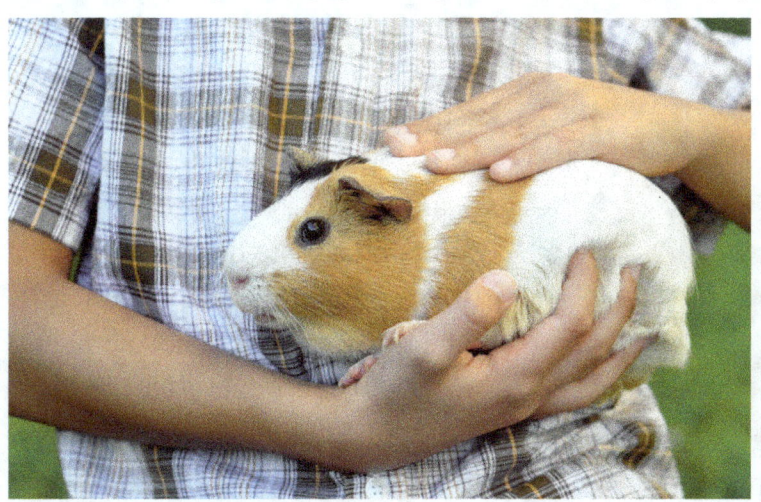

You'll discover that these animals have distinct personalities and complex social relationships. Some guinea pigs are natural leaders who organize the group, others are gentle followers who prefer peace and quiet, and many are little entertainers who seem to perform just to make their families laugh. Watching two or more guinea pigs interact teaches you about friendship, communication, and cooperation in ways you never expected.

Did You Know? Guinea pigs got their name from early traders who sold them for a guinea (an old British coin)—they're not from Guinea and they're not pigs!

Guinea pig ownership becomes a daily adventure in understanding animal behavior, developing empathy, and experiencing the satisfaction of providing excellent care for creatures who genuinely appreciate your efforts.

1.2 Guinea Pig Breeds and Coat Types Made Simple

Not all guinea pigs are created equal! While they may look similar at first glance, different breeds have very different care requirements, grooming needs, and personality traits. Understanding these differences helps you choose guinea pigs that will thrive in your family's specific situation.

American Guinea Pigs: The Perfect Beginners

American guinea pigs (also called English guinea pigs) are the classic, short-haired variety that most people picture when they think of guinea pigs. At 1-3 pounds and 8-10 inches long, they're sturdy, manageable pets with smooth, dense coats that lie flat against their bodies.

Why families love American guinea pigs: Their short coats require minimal grooming—just occasional brushing and regular health checks. They're generally calm and easy to handle, making them ideal for first-time guinea pig families. Their coats come in dozens of color combinations, from solid colors to beautiful patterns like tortoiseshell, brindle, and Dutch markings.

American guinea pig care: These pigs are relatively low-maintenance compared to long-haired breeds. Weekly brushing helps remove loose fur and keeps their coats shiny. They're excellent choices for busy families or those new to guinea pig care.

Long-Haired Breeds: The Glamorous Beauties

Long-haired guinea pigs are absolutely stunning but require significantly more grooming commitment. The two most common long-haired breeds have distinct care needs:

Peruvian Guinea Pigs have the longest coats of all breeds, with hair that can grow up to 20 inches long if left untrimmed. Their hair grows continuously and flows in all directions, creating a dramatic, flowing appearance. However, this beauty comes with daily grooming requirements.

Silkie Guinea Pigs (also called Sheltie guinea pigs) have long, soft hair that grows backward from their head, creating a more manageable coat than Peruvians. Their hair is silky smooth and doesn't grow quite as long, but still requires regular attention.

Long-haired care requirements: Daily brushing is essential to prevent painful mats and tangles. Many families choose to trim the coats shorter for easier maintenance. These breeds need more frequent baths and careful attention to keeping bedding clean. They're best for experienced families who enjoy the grooming process.

Abyssinian Guinea Pigs: The Unique Personalities

Abyssinian guinea pigs are instantly recognizable by their distinctive "rosettes"—circular cowlicks of hair that create natural patterns across their bodies. A show-quality Abyssinian has eight to ten rosettes in specific locations, creating a coat that looks almost like it's been styled.

Abyssinian characteristics: Beyond their unique appearance, many Abyssinian guinea pigs have particularly outgoing, mischievous personalities. They're often described as the "clowns" of the guinea pig world, with curious, active temperaments that keep families entertained.

Care considerations: Their textured coats need regular brushing to prevent matting where rosettes meet. They're generally easier to maintain than long-haired breeds but require more grooming than smooth Americans.

Rex Guinea Pigs: The Teddy Bears

Rex guinea pigs have dense, curly coats that feel like soft wool. Their hair is shorter than long-haired breeds but much denser than Americans, creating a plush, teddy bear-like texture that many people find irresistible to touch.

Rex breed traits: Their coats don't require extensive grooming, but they do need regular brushing to keep the curls from matting. Many Rex guinea pigs have particularly gentle, calm personalities that make them excellent pets for children.

Skinny Pigs: The Special Needs Beauties

Skinny pigs are essentially hairless guinea pigs with only small patches of hair on their noses, feet, and legs. While they're not technically a different species, they have significantly different care requirements that make them best suited for experienced guinea pig families.

Special care needs: Skinny pigs require temperature-controlled environments since they can't regulate body heat like furred guinea pigs. They need protection from both cold and sun exposure, special attention to skin care, and sometimes require sweaters or heating in cool weather.

Personality traits: Many skinny pig enthusiasts report that these animals have particularly social, outgoing personalities, perhaps because they seek warmth and contact more actively than furred varieties.

1.3 The Guinea Pig Commitment Check ✅

Before you fall completely in love with the idea of guinea pig ownership, let's have an honest conversation about what you're committing to. This isn't meant to discourage you—it's designed to ensure you're prepared for success with these wonderful but complex pets.

Time: Your Daily and Weekly Investment

Daily commitment (20-30 minutes):

- Morning check-in: Fresh vegetables, hay refill, quick health observation (10 minutes)

- Evening interaction: Pellet feeding, fresh water, gentle handling or floor time (15-20 minutes)

- Spot cleaning: Removing soiled bedding from eating and high-traffic areas (5 minutes)

Weekly commitment (45-60 minutes):

• Thorough cage cleaning: Complete bedding change, accessory cleaning, habitat maintenance

• Health monitoring: Weighing, nail trimming (as needed), checking for any changes in behavior or appearance

• Supply management: Restocking hay, pellets, vegetables, and bedding

• Social time: Extended floor time or bonding sessions

Space: What Your Guinea Pigs Really Need

Minimum habitat requirements:

• Single guinea pig: 7.5 square feet of floor space (30" x 36" minimum)

• Pair of guinea pigs: 10.5 square feet of floor space (30" x 50" minimum)

• Three or more: Add 2-3 square feet per additional guinea pig

• Ceiling height: At least 14 inches for jumping and standing

• Multiple levels are helpful but don't count toward minimum floor space

Beyond the habitat, you'll need space for:

FUN FACT
Guinea pigs love to zoom and popcorn (little happy jumps) when they have lots of space in their cage!

• Supply storage for hay (takes up significant space), vegetables, pellets, and cleaning supplies

• Floor time play area—guinea pigs need daily exercise outside their habitat

• Temporary housing during cleaning

• Veterinary carrier for transport

Financial Reality: Setup and Ongoing Costs

Starting costs for a proper two-guinea-pig setup include an appropriate-sized habitat (C&C cage or large commercial cage), initial bedding supply (fleece system or disposable bedding), food and water supplies (heavy bowls, large water bottles), hay supply and storage, quality pellets and initial vegetable variety, hideouts, toys, and enrichment items, plus first veterinary checkups for both guinea pigs. Plan to spend about as much as a good bicycle for the complete initial setup for two guinea pigs.

Monthly ongoing costs include fresh hay (guinea pigs eat lots of hay!), daily fresh vegetables, quality pellets, bedding materials or fleece washing, occasional veterinary care, and replacement toys and enrichment. This usually costs about the same as a family restaurant dinner each month.

The 6-8 Year Journey

Guinea pigs typically live 6-8 years with excellent care, which represents a significant commitment that spans major life changes for families.

Are You Ready? Interactive Family Checklist

Work through this checklist together as a family. Be honest—your future guinea pigs depend on it!

Housing and Space

☐ We have identified a suitable location for a guinea pig habitat
☐ We have space for proper-sized habitat (minimum 7.5 sq ft for one, 10.5 for pair)
☐ We can provide daily floor time in a safe, guinea pig-proofed area
☐ We have considered noise levels (guinea pigs are vocal, especially during feeding)
☐ We have adequate storage space for hay and supplies

Time and Commitment

☐ Someone in our family is available for daily care (morning and evening routines)
☐ We can commit to weekly deep cleaning (45-60 minutes every week)
☐ We understand this is a 6-8 year commitment and are prepared for the full lifespan
☐ We have a plan for vacation and emergency care
☐ We're prepared to care for multiple guinea pigs (pairs or groups)

Financial Readiness

☐ We have budgeted for initial setup costs (about the cost of a good bicycle)
☐ We can afford monthly ongoing expenses (about the cost of a family restaurant dinner)
☐ We have funds set aside for potential veterinary emergencies
☐ We understand that costs continue even if interest decreases
☐ We've budgeted for caring for at least two guinea pigs

Knowledge and Preparation

☐ We have researched guinea pig care requirements (you're doing this now!)
☐ We have located an exotic pet veterinarian in our area
☐ We understand breed differences and grooming requirements
☐ We have realistic expectations about handling, social needs, and guinea pig behavior
☐ We understand the importance of pairs and social companionship

Family Agreement

☐ All family members are enthusiastic about the decision
☐ We have discussed primary caretaker responsibilities (with parent oversight)
☐ We understand that parents are ultimately responsible for pet welfare
☐ We have discussed what happens if circumstances change (moving, allergies, loss of interest)
☐ We're committed to providing excellent care for 6-8 years

For children: A guinea pig adopted in 4th grade will likely be a companion through high school. This long relationship allows for deep bonding but also requires sustained commitment through changing interests and responsibilities.

For families: You're committing to consistent care through multiple school years, family moves, vacations, and schedule changes. The longer lifespan means more total investment but also more years of companionship and learning.

Family Readiness Assessment

Physical readiness:

- Can family members safely lift and support guinea pigs for handling?
- Are children old enough to understand gentle handling requirements?
- Does anyone in the household have allergies to hay, guinea pigs, or bedding materials?
- Can the family manage daily vegetable preparation and regular cage cleaning?

Emotional and social readiness:

- Are you prepared for the natural cycle of pet ownership, including end-of-life care for animals with 6-8 year lifespans?
- Can you provide consistent care even when the novelty wears off?
- Will you be able to find appropriate care during vacations or family emergencies?
- Are all family members genuinely enthusiastic about caring for multiple pets?

Space and lifestyle compatibility:

- Do you have adequate space for the minimum habitat requirements?
- Can you accommodate the daily floor time needs?
- Is your household generally calm enough for guinea pigs (they're sensitive to stress and loud noises)?

- Do you have realistic expectations about noise levels (guinea pigs can be quite vocal, especially at feeding times)?

What If You're Not Ready Yet?

If you didn't check every box, that's perfectly okay! It's much better to wait until you're truly prepared than to get guinea pigs and discover you're overwhelmed. Consider waiting until after a major family transition, until children are slightly older and more capable of consistent care, until you have more predictable schedules and routines, or until you've saved enough for both setup and emergency costs.

When You're Ready to Move Forward

If you checked all the boxes and feel confident about proceeding, congratulations! You're demonstrating the kind of thoughtful, responsible approach that leads to successful guinea pig ownership.

Your next step is understanding why guinea pigs do best with companions and learning how to plan for pairs. In Chapter 2, we'll explore the social nature of guinea pigs and help you understand why "two is better than one" isn't just a nice idea—it's essential for their mental and emotional health.

••

Coming up in Chapter 2: Learn why guinea pigs are social animals who need companionship, how to choose compatible pairs, and what it means to plan for multiple pets from the very beginning of your guinea pig journey.

Chapter 2:
Why Two Is Better Than One

2.1 Understanding Guinea Pig Social Needs

Here's something that might surprise you: in the wild, guinea pigs live in groups of 10-20 animals, creating complex social networks with friendships, communication systems, and cooperative behaviors. When we bring guinea pigs into our homes as single pets, we're asking them to live in a way that goes against everything that comes naturally to them.

This doesn't mean guinea pig ownership is wrong—it means we need to understand their deep need for companionship and plan accordingly. A single guinea pig can become lonely, stressed, and even develop behavioral problems, no matter how much human attention they receive. We simply can't replace the specific type of companionship that another guinea pig provides.

The Science Behind Social Needs

Guinea pigs are prey animals who developed complex social behaviors for survival. In their natural habitat, they rely on group members for warning calls about predators, cooperative foraging for food, social grooming that maintains health and relationships, and emotional comfort during stressful times.

When guinea pigs are housed alone, they miss out on these essential interactions. Even the most dedicated human family cannot provide the specific types of communication, physical contact, and social learning that guinea pigs get from their own species.

FUN FACT

In the wild, guinea pig groups have "sentries" who watch for danger while others eat—they take turns being the lookout!

Research consistently shows that guinea pigs in pairs or small groups show less stress-related behaviors, are more active and playful, live longer, healthier lives, display more natural behaviors, and are actually easier for families to care for because they entertain each other.

What Guinea Pig Friendship Looks Like

Watching bonded guinea pigs interact teaches you about friendship in ways you never expected. You'll see them sharing food, with one guinea pig stepping back to let their friend eat first. They groom each other, focusing on areas that are hard to reach alone—especially around the ears and neck.

Bonded guinea pigs often sleep curled up together, creating adorable piggy pile-ups that provide warmth and security. They communicate constantly through soft chirps, purrs, and body language that shows affection and reassurance.

When one guinea pig is scared, their companion often moves closer to provide comfort. When one is excited about something, the enthusiasm spreads to their friend. This emotional connection enriches their lives in ways that no amount of human interaction can fully replace.

Common Myths About Single Guinea Pigs

Myth: "One guinea pig will bond more closely with humans."

Reality: Guinea pigs with companions often become more confident and social with humans because they feel more secure. A stressed, lonely guinea pig may actually be more withdrawn from human interaction.

Myth: "Two guinea pigs are twice as much work."

Reality: Paired guinea pigs often require less human entertainment time because they provide mental stimulation for each other. They're generally happier and healthier, which can actually mean fewer behavioral problems and health issues.

Myth: "My family can provide enough social interaction."

Reality: Even the most dedicated family cannot provide 24-hour companionship. Guinea pigs are most active during times when families are often busy with work, school, and other activities.

Myth: "I'll get a second guinea pig later if my first one seems lonely."

Reality: While introductions can work, it's much easier to adopt a bonded pair or introduce two young guinea pigs simultaneously. Established territorial behaviors can make later introductions more challenging.

2.2 Benefits of Pairs vs. Single Guinea Pigs

The advantages of keeping guinea pigs in pairs extend far beyond meeting their social needs—they impact every aspect of care and create a more rewarding experience for your family.

Emotional and Behavioral Benefits

Reduced anxiety: Guinea pigs in pairs show significantly less stress-related behaviors like excessive hiding, repetitive movements, or aggressive responses to handling. They feel more secure with a companion nearby.

Natural communication: Paired guinea pigs constantly "talk" to each other through squeaks, purrs, and body language. This communication keeps their social skills sharp and provides mental stimulation that no toy can replace.

Confidence building: Guinea pigs often learn from each other. A shy guinea pig may become more adventurous by following a confident companion, while bold guinea pigs may learn caution from more careful friends.

Play and entertainment: Bonded guinea pigs chase each other, play gentle games, and engage in behaviors that solo guinea pigs rarely display. Watching these interactions provides endless entertainment for families.

Health and Wellness Advantages

Social grooming: Guinea pigs clean each other's ears, faces, and hard-to-reach spots, improving hygiene and health. This grooming also helps detect health problems early when one guinea pig notices changes in their companion.

Exercise motivation: Paired guinea pigs are generally more active because they encourage each other to explore, run, and play. This increased activity promotes better physical health and weight management.

Stress reduction: Lower stress levels support stronger immune systems and better overall health. Guinea pigs with companions typically have fewer stress-related health issues.

Appetite regulation: Guinea pigs often eat better in pairs because feeding becomes a social activity. They encourage each other to try new foods and maintain healthy eating patterns.

Family Benefits

Doubled entertainment: Two guinea pig personalities mean twice the cute behaviors, funny interactions, and adorable moments for your family to enjoy.

Teaching opportunities: Watching guinea pig social dynamics teaches children about friendship, communication, cooperation, and conflict resolution in ways that single pets cannot.

Easier care routines: Paired guinea pigs often have synchronized schedules and routines, making care more predictable and efficient for busy families.

Reduced guilt: Knowing your guinea pigs have companionship when you're at school or work eliminates the worry about lonely pets waiting at home.

2.3 Choosing Compatible Pairs

Not all guinea pig combinations work equally well. Understanding compatibility factors helps ensure harmonious relationships that last throughout your pets' lives.

Same-Sex Pairs: The Foundation of Success

Female pairs (sows): Female guinea pigs typically form the most stable, long-lasting friendships. They rarely show serious aggression toward each other and often develop deeply bonded relationships that last their entire lives.

Advantages of female pairs:

- Generally peaceful and cooperative
- Less territorial than males
- Easier to introduce and maintain
- Can often be kept in groups of three or more

> **QUICK TIP**
> *Avoid pairing two male guinea pigs in a small cage. They may fight over territory and space.*

Male pairs (boars): Male guinea pigs can form excellent friendships, but they require more careful selection and introduction. Successfully bonded male pairs often become incredibly close companions.

Considerations for male pairs:

- Need adequate space to establish separate territories

- Work best when introduced as young guinea pigs
- May require larger habitats than female pairs
- Should be neutered if housed with females

Age Considerations

Young pairs: Baby guinea pigs (under 4 months) typically adapt to each other most easily and form the strongest bonds. If you're adopting from a breeder or rescue, young pairs are often the ideal choice.

Adult pairs: Adult guinea pigs can certainly form friendships, but introductions require more patience and careful supervision. Many rescues have bonded adult pairs available for adoption.

Mixed ages: Sometimes older guinea pigs accept younger companions, but this pairing requires careful monitoring to ensure the older guinea pig doesn't bully or overwhelm the younger one.

Personality Matching

Energy levels: Guinea pigs with similar activity levels often get along better than those with very different energy levels. A very active guinea pig might overwhelm a calm, quiet companion.

Dominance patterns: Every guinea pig pair will establish a gentle dominance hierarchy, which is normal and healthy. However, pairs work best when dominance differences aren't extreme.

Sociability: Some guinea pigs are naturally more social and outgoing, while others are shy and reserved. Mixed personality pairs can work, but similar temperaments often create more harmonious relationships.

What to Avoid

Male-female pairs: Unless you want baby guinea pigs, avoid opposite-sex pairs. Guinea pigs reproduce frequently and easily, and pregnancy/birthing carries risks for female guinea pigs.

Large groups initially: While guinea pigs can live in groups, start with pairs and add additional guinea pigs only after the first pair is well-established and you've gained experience.

FUN FACT
Guinea pigs sleep in "shifts"—one often stays alert while the other naps.

Unrelated adults from different sources: It's much easier to introduce guinea pigs who have some familiarity with each other than to combine completely strange adults.

2.4 Introduction Techniques and Quarantine Procedures

Successfully introducing guinea pigs requires patience, preparation, and understanding of guinea pig social dynamics. Rushing introductions can create lasting problems, while careful, gradual approaches usually result in lifelong friendships.

The Importance of Quarantine

Before introducing any new guinea pig to your home, a quarantine period protects both your existing pets and new arrivals from potential health problems.

Quarantine setup: House new guinea pigs in a completely separate room from existing pets for 2-3 weeks. Use separate supplies and equipment when caring for quarantined animals.

What to watch for: Monitor new guinea pigs for signs of respiratory infections, digestive problems, parasites, or behavioral issues that might affect successful introductions.

Veterinary checkups: Schedule examinations for all guinea pigs before introductions. This ensures everyone is healthy and up-to-date on preventive care.

Gradual Introduction Process

Step 1: Scent Introduction (Days 1-3): Place the guinea pigs in cages near each other but not touching. They can smell and hear each other without direct contact. Watch for curiosity rather than aggression or fear.

Step 2: Visual Contact (Days 4-7): Allow the guinea pigs to see each other through cage bars or clear barriers. Positive signs include approaching the barrier, gentle squeaking, or relaxed body postures.

Step 3: Neutral Territory Meeting (Day 8+): Conduct first face-to-face meetings in a space that neither guinea pig considers their territory. A bathroom floor or large exercise pen works well.

Step 4: Supervised Interactions: Allow increasingly longer supervised meetings in neutral territory. Provide multiple hideouts, food sources, and escape routes during these sessions.

Step 5: Cohabitation Trial: Once guinea pigs show consistently friendly behavior, try housing them together in a thoroughly cleaned habitat with new bedding and rearranged accessories.

Reading Introduction Body Language

Positive signs:

- Approaching each other willingly
- Gentle sniffing and investigation
- Sharing food or water sources
- Resting near each other
- Soft chattering or purring sounds

Warning signs:

- Teeth chattering or aggressive vocalizations
- Raised fur or arched backs
- Blocking access to food, water, or hideouts
- Chasing that doesn't end in play
- Persistent mounting or dominance displays

FUN FACT
Bonded pairs will "call" to each other if separated even briefly.

When to separate: If guinea pigs show sustained aggression, draw blood, or seem genuinely fearful after multiple introduction attempts, they may not be compatible. This is disappointment but not failure—some guinea pigs simply prefer different companions.

2.5 When Single Guinea Pigs Work (Rare Exceptions)

While pairs are strongly recommended for almost all situations, very specific circumstances might make single guinea pig ownership appropriate.

Medical Exceptions

Severe illness: Guinea pigs with certain contagious conditions may need isolation during treatment. However, the goal should be reunification with companions once health permits.

Age-related issues: Very elderly guinea pigs who have lost companions may be too frail for the stress of new introductions. In these cases, extra human attention becomes crucial.

Aggressive individuals: Rarely, individual guinea pigs may be too aggressive for safe cohabitation despite proper introduction attempts. These animals need extensive enrichment and interaction to prevent loneliness.

Temporary Situations

Transition periods: Guinea pigs between companions (due to loss or rehoming) may be temporarily single while new partnerships are arranged.

Specialized care: Guinea pigs recovering from surgery or serious illness may need temporary isolation but should be reunited with companions as soon as medically appropriate.

Maximizing Single Guinea Pig Welfare

If circumstances require single guinea pig housing, extraordinary measures become necessary:

Increased human interaction: Single guinea pigs need multiple daily interaction sessions with their human families to provide some social stimulation.

Enhanced enrichment: Provide extra toys, hiding places, and environmental complexity to combat boredom and loneliness.

Consistent routines: Predictable schedules become more important for single guinea pigs who lack the comfort of constant companionship.

Future planning: Always keep the goal of eventual companionship in mind and be prepared to add a compatible partner when circumstances allow.

2.6 Planning for Your Guinea Pig Family

Caring for guinea pig pairs means thinking bigger—more space, more supplies, and more budget—but the rewards of watching bonded guinea pigs live their best lives together make every bit of extra planning worthwhile.

Space Planning for Happy Pairs

The bigger picture: Guinea pig pairs need significantly more room than you might expect. Think "guinea pig apartment" rather than "guinea pig bedroom"—they need space to have their own territories while still enjoying each other's company.

Beyond just floor space: Your guinea pig pair will need multiple hideouts so they can have alone time when they want it, several food and water spots to prevent dinner arguments, plenty of floor time space for exercise and exploration together, and extra storage for all those supplies (guinea pigs eat a lot!).

The Money Reality Check

Setup costs scale up: Everything gets bigger and more expensive when you're planning for two guinea pigs. Larger habitats, double the accessories, bigger initial supply orders, and vet checkups for both guinea pigs add up quickly.

Monthly costs multiply: Two guinea pigs eat about twice as much food (shocking, right?), create more mess requiring more bedding, need more toys since they're harder on equipment together, and both need veterinary care throughout their lives.

Smart money moves: Buy hay and bedding in bulk when you can afford it, connect with other guinea pig families to share large purchases, look for bonded pairs from rescues (often less expensive than separate adoptions), and build your setup gradually rather than buying everything at once.

Time Investment That Pays Off

The good news: Paired guinea pigs often make your life easier in some ways. They entertain each other, follow similar schedules, and need less individual human attention than lonely single guinea pigs.

The reality check: Two guinea pigs mean bigger cleaning jobs, more complex health monitoring (watching two different personalities and health patterns), and more supply management (you'll go through food and bedding faster than you expect).

Why it's worth it: Families who provide proper companionship for their guinea pigs consistently report happier, healthier pets with fewer behavioral problems and more entertaining daily interactions.

The investment in doing guinea pig ownership right from the beginning—including proper companionship—creates the foundation for years of rewarding experiences with pets who truly thrive in your care.

· ·

Coming up in Chapter 3: Learn how to set up the perfect habitat for your guinea pig pair or group, including choosing between C&C cages and commercial options, creating indoor and outdoor environments, and providing all the essential features that make guinea pigs thrive.

Chapter 3: Setting Up Your Guinea Pig's Dream Home

3.1 Choosing the Right Home Size

Imagine trying to live your entire life in your bedroom—never leaving, never having space to run or explore. That's exactly what happens when guinea pigs are kept in homes that are too small. The most important decision you'll make for your guinea pigs' happiness is choosing a home that gives them space to run, explore, socialize, and simply be guinea pigs.

Here's something many pet stores won't tell you: Most guinea pig cages sold in stores are too small. Those colorful plastic cages with multiple levels might look appealing, but they often provide less than half the floor space your guinea pigs actually need for healthy, natural behaviors.

FUN FACT
Guinea pigs love to play hide-and-seek! Adding tunnels, huts, and hidey houses to their cage makes them feel safe and keeps them entertained.

The Science Behind Space Requirements

Minimum space requirements based on current research:

- Single guinea pig: 7.5 square feet of continuous floor space
- Pair of guinea pigs: 10.5 square feet of continuous floor space
- Three guinea pigs: 13 square feet of continuous floor space
- Four guinea pigs: 16 square feet of continuous floor space

Why these numbers matter: In the wild, guinea pigs live in large social groups that roam territories covering several acres. While we can't replicate that exact environment, providing adequate space allows them to express natural behaviors like running in straight lines rather than just circles, establishing separate areas for eating, sleeping, and elimination, creating social spaces and private retreats, and engaging in normal social interactions without constant crowding.

Understanding "floor space": Don't count upper levels in multi-level cages toward minimum space requirements because guinea pigs are ground-dwelling animals who need room to run horizontally. Vertical space is nice for climbing and variety, but it doesn't replace adequate floor area.

3.2 Housing Options That Actually Work

The good news is that creating an amazing guinea pig home doesn't require expensive specialty equipment. Some of the best guinea pig habitats are built by families using creative, budget-friendly solutions.

C&C Cages: The Popular Choice

C&C cages (Cubes and Coroplast) have become the favorite choice for many guinea pig families because they're customizable, affordable, and give your guinea pigs exactly the space they need.

What makes C&C cages great: You can build exactly the size your guinea pigs need, expand easily if you add more guinea pigs later, cost much less than huge commercial cages, and clean more easily than complex multi-level setups.

Basic C&C setup: Wire storage cube panels connect to form walls, while a plastic bottom (coroplast) creates the floor. You can find supplies at office stores, online, or from companies that sell complete kits.

Simple C&C sizes that work: • 2x4 grids: Perfect for two guinea pigs (about 10.5 square feet) • 2x5 grids: Comfortable for two, minimum for three guinea pigs • 2x6 grids: Spacious for three guinea pigs

Large Commercial Cages

If you prefer ready-made solutions, some commercial cages work well for guinea pig pairs when chosen carefully.

What to look for: Floor space that meets your guinea pigs' needs, deep bases that contain bedding and messes, wide doors for easy cleaning and guinea pig access, and sturdy construction that won't wobble or tip.

Commercial cage reality check: Good commercial cages that are actually large enough for guinea pig pairs cost significantly more than C&C alternatives. However, they're ready to use immediately and don't require assembly skills.

Outdoor Housing

Unlike hamsters, guinea pigs can live outdoors in properly built hutches during appropriate weather. However, outdoor housing requires extra planning for safety and comfort.

Outdoor benefits: More space possibilities, fresh air and natural environment, and often less expensive than large indoor setups.

Outdoor challenges: Weather protection needs, predator safety requirements, and more complex daily care routines.

Essential outdoor features: Weatherproof sleeping areas, predator-proof construction with secure latches, proper ventilation without drafts, and raised construction to prevent dampness.

Seasonal considerations: Summer requires shade and cooling options, winter needs insulation and wind protection, and year-round requires backup indoor housing for extreme weather.

3.2 Essential Features for Happy Guinea Pigs

Regardless of which housing option you choose, certain features make the difference between a guinea pig house and a guinea pig home.

Flooring That Works

Fleece bedding systems: Many guinea pig families love fleece because it's soft, reusable, and cost-effective over time. Fleece wicks moisture away from guinea pigs while absorbent layers underneath soak up liquids.

Fleece advantages: Comfortable for guinea pig feet, environmentally friendly, and allows easy health monitoring since you can see elimination patterns clearly.

Fleece requirements: Multiple fleece sets for washing rotation, absorbent layers (towels or special liners), and commitment to regular washing every 3-4 days.

Traditional bedding: Paper-based bedding, aspen shavings, or hemp bedding work well for families who prefer disposable options.

Bedding advantages: Simple to change and dispose, familiar to guinea pigs, and no laundry requirements.

Bedding to avoid: Cedar or pine shavings (can cause breathing problems), corn cob bedding (can cause blockages if eaten), and fluffy materials that could be dangerous if consumed.

Multiple Hideouts and Security

Guinea pigs are prey animals who need safe spaces where they can retreat when feeling vulnerable. Multiple hideouts also let pairs have their own territories while sharing the same home.

Hideout essentials: One hideout per guinea pig plus one extra, multiple entrances so guinea pigs don't get trapped, appropriate sizing (big enough to turn around but cozy enough to feel secure), and easy cleaning access.

Great hideout options: Wooden houses from pet stores, cardboard boxes (free and replaceable!), plastic igloos designed for guinea pigs, and ceramic or wooden tunnels.

Food and Water Setup

Food containers: Heavy ceramic bowls that won't tip over, separate bowls for pellets and fresh vegetables, and wide, shallow designs for easy guinea pig access.

Water options: Large water bottles (16+ ounces for pairs) with secure mounting, or heavy ceramic water bowls that won't tip. Some guinea pigs prefer drinking from bowls, while others like bottles better.

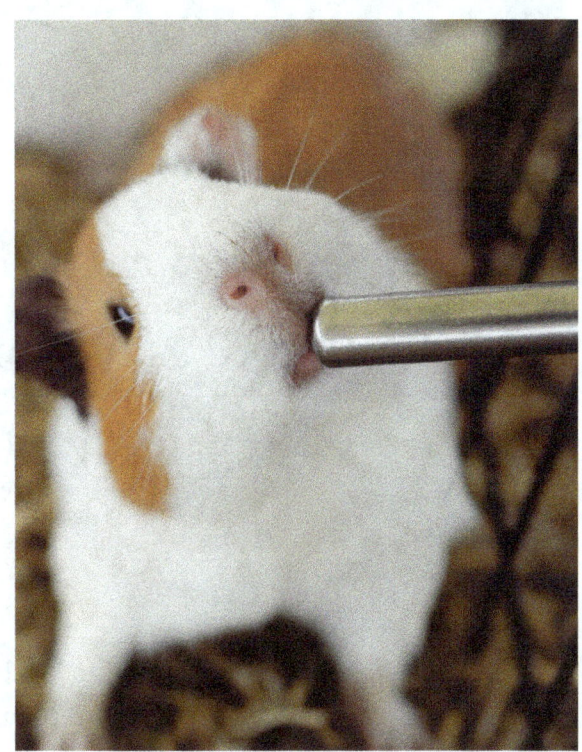

Hay management: Hay racks that keep hay clean and accessible, or simply scatter hay in multiple locations around the habitat. Guinea pigs eat lots of hay, so they need constant access.

3.3 Creating the Perfect Environment

Beyond basic housing, a few environmental factors make huge differences in your guinea pigs' daily comfort and health.

Temperature and Climate

Ideal temperature range: 65-75°F (18-24°C)

Why temperature matters: Guinea pigs are sensitive to both heat and cold. Too hot (above 80°F) can cause dangerous overheating, while too cold (below 60°F) can make them sick.

Summer cooling: Provide ceramic tiles for guinea pigs to lie on, ensure good air circulation, and never place habitats in direct sunlight or near heat sources.

Winter warmth: Avoid drafts while maintaining fresh air, provide extra bedding for comfort, and consider safe supplemental heating if your house gets very cold.

Enrichment That Makes a Difference

Mental stimulation essentials: Safe chew toys (apple wood, willow branches), tunnels and tubes for exploration, platforms and ramps for climbing, and hiding spots where you can scatter food for foraging fun.

Rotation keeps things interesting: Change toys weekly to maintain novelty, use seasonal themes with safe natural materials, and create simple DIY enrichment using cardboard boxes, paper bags, and toilet paper tubes.

Exercise opportunities: Guinea pigs need daily floor time outside their habitat for exercise and exploration. Plan for a safe, guinea pig-proofed area where they can run and play.

3.4 Shopping Smart: Budget-Friendly Setup

Setting up guinea pig housing can be expensive, but smart shopping strategies help you provide excellent care while managing costs.

Money-Saving Strategies

DIY solutions: Build C&C cages instead of buying expensive commercial options, create hideouts from cardboard boxes or wooden crates, and make toys from safe household materials like toilet paper tubes.

QUICK TIP
Skip fancy toys! Guinea pigs are just as happy with simple cardboard boxes and paper bags, which make great hideouts and cost almost nothing.

> ## Essential Items Checklist ✅
>
> **Must-have items before bringing your guinea pigs home:**
>
> - **Housing:** Proper-sized habitat (C&C cage materials or large commercial cage meeting space requirements), appropriate flooring system (fleece setup or quality bedding), and secure setup that prevents escapes.
>
> - **Food and Water:** Heavy ceramic food bowls that won't tip over, large water bottles (16+ oz) or ceramic water bowls, timothy hay supply with storage container, and high-quality guinea pig pellets (2-3 pound bag).
>
> - **Comfort and Safety:** Multiple hideouts (one per guinea pig plus extra), safe chew toys made from appropriate woods, and fresh vegetable starter variety for daily salads.
>
> - **Emergency/Health:** Small pet carrier large enough for guinea pig pairs, kitchen scale for weekly weight monitoring, and basic first aid supplies including styptic powder for nail trimming accidents.

Smart shopping: Buy hay and bedding in bulk when possible, shop sales for fleece and towels, and connect with other guinea pig families to share bulk purchases.

Gradual building: Start with essentials and add enrichment items over time rather than buying everything at once.

Budget-Friendly Setup Plans

Starter setup: C&C cage with basic materials, simple fleece system or quality bedding, essential food and water supplies, cardboard hideouts, and basic hay and pellet supply.

Enhanced setup: Larger C&C system, multiple fleece sets for easy washing, variety of commercial and DIY hideouts, premium food varieties, and comprehensive toy selection.

Remember: the most expensive setup isn't necessarily the best if it doesn't match your family's actual needs and maintenance abilities. Focus on providing adequate space, good nutrition, and genuine care rather than accumulating expensive accessories.

Your guinea pigs will be much happier with a simple setup that gets excellent daily care than a fancy habitat that's difficult to maintain properly. The time and love you invest in their daily care matters far more than expensive equipment.

Creating the perfect guinea pig habitat is about understanding their needs and working within your family's circumstances to meet those needs creatively and consistently.

··

Coming up in Chapter 4: Learn the step-by-step process of choosing and bringing your guinea pigs home, from selecting healthy, compatible pairs to managing those crucial first weeks that set the foundation for lifelong relationships.

Chapter 4: Bringing Your Guinea Pigs Home

4.1 Choosing Your Guinea Pigs

The moment you've been preparing for has arrived—it's time to choose your guinea pigs! This decision will shape your family's experience for the next 6-8 years, so let's make sure you know exactly what to look for and what questions to ask.

What Healthy Guinea Pigs Look Like

Finding healthy guinea pigs is like being a detective—you're looking for clues that tell you these animals have been well cared for and are ready to thrive in your home.

Happy, healthy guinea pigs have bright, clear eyes that follow movement and show curiosity about what's happening around them. Their noses should be clean and only slightly moist from normal sniffing and exploring. A good coat looks full and glossy, lying smooth against their body (unless they're a breed with naturally textured fur).

Check their body condition by looking for guinea pigs who appear well-fed but not overweight. They should move around easily and comfortably, without limping or seeming stiff. Healthy guinea pigs also keep themselves clean—their bottoms should be dry and their overall appearance neat.

Listen to their sounds too! Healthy guinea pigs often make soft conversational sounds with each other and may wheek with excitement if they think food is coming. Any guinea pig making obvious distress sounds or breathing noisily needs veterinary attention.

> ▶ **Red flags to avoid:** Trust your instincts! If something seems "off" about the guinea pigs you're considering, listen to that feeling.
>
> **Signs that should make you look elsewhere** include guinea pigs who seem extremely lethargic or uninterested in their surroundings, obvious breathing problems like wheezing or mouth breathing, dirty, smelly living conditions that suggest poor care, and aggressive behavior that goes beyond normal territorial displays.
>
> **Also avoid** guinea pigs with visible injuries that aren't being treated, overgrown nails or teeth suggesting neglect, and any situation where staff can't or won't answer basic questions about the animals' care and history.

Age Matters: Young vs. Adult Guinea Pigs

Baby guinea pigs (8-12 weeks) are absolutely adorable and adapt quickly to new families. They're like little sponges, learning about their world and bonding easily with gentle families. However, young guinea pigs need more frequent feeding and extra-careful handling since they're still growing.

Adult guinea pigs (4 months-3 years) often make wonderful family pets because their personalities are already established. What you see is what you get! Adult guinea pigs from good sources are usually calmer and easier to handle, though they might take a little longer to fully trust their new families.

Senior guinea pigs (4+ years) can be incredibly rewarding pets for families who want to provide loving care for animals in their golden years. These guinea pigs often have gentle, grateful personalities and form deep bonds with families who give them comfort and security.

4.2 Where to Find Your Guinea Pigs
Rescue Organizations: Heroes for Guinea Pigs

Many amazing guinea pigs end up in rescue organizations through no fault of their own—family moves, allergies, or simply people who didn't understand what guinea pig care required. Adopting from rescue organizations often means getting guinea pigs who are already bonded pairs, have known health history, and come with ongoing support.

Great rescue organizations will ask you lots of questions about your prepared setup and commitment level. Don't be offended—they're making sure you and the guinea pigs are a good match! They often provide spay/neuter services, initial veterinary care, and will take the guinea pigs back if your circumstances change.

QUICK TIP
Long-haired breeds are beautiful, but they need extra grooming. Choose short-haired if you want easier care.

Questions to ask rescues: "What do you know about these guinea pigs' personalities and history?" "Have they been examined by a veterinarian recently?" "What food and care routine have they been following?" "Do you provide ongoing support after adoption?"

Ethical Breeders: When You Want Specific Traits

Good breeders focus on health, temperament, and proper care rather than just producing lots of baby guinea pigs. They usually have fewer animals, know the parents' health history, and provide early socialization that helps guinea pigs become confident pets.

Quality breeders will want to meet your family and see that you're prepared for guinea pig ownership. They should be happy to show you their facilities, answer detailed questions, and provide health records for parent animals.

Questions for breeders: "Can I meet the parent guinea pigs?" "What health testing do you do?" "How do you socialize baby guinea pigs?" "What happens if we can't keep these guinea pigs in the future?"

Pet Stores: Choose Very Carefully

Some pet stores provide excellent care for their animals and work with local rescues, while others focus more on quick sales than animal welfare. If you choose to adopt from a pet store, evaluate their practices carefully.

Good pet stores have clean, spacious enclosures with proper group housing (same-sex pairs or groups), knowledgeable staff who can answer detailed care questions, relationships with local veterinarians for animal health care, and willingness to let you observe guinea pigs before making decisions.

Avoid pet stores with overcrowded, dirty conditions, staff who can't answer basic guinea pig care questions, mixed-sex housing that suggests unplanned breeding, or high-pressure sales tactics that discourage careful consideration.

4.3 The Journey Home

Getting your guinea pigs safely from their current location to your prepared home is their first big adventure together. How you handle this trip can set the tone for your entire relationship.

Safe Transport for Guinea Pig Pairs

Choose the right carrier for your guinea pig pair. They need enough space to sit comfortably together (bonded pairs travel better together), adequate ventilation without drafts, and secure latches that guinea pigs can't open but you can access quickly if needed.

Make the carrier comfortable with a small amount of familiar bedding from their previous location, enough hay for comfort chewing during the journey, and a towel covering part of the carrier to reduce visual stress while maintaining airflow.

Travel Tips That Reduce Stress

In the car, place the carrier securely on the floor where it won't slide around, maintain comfortable temperature without direct air conditioning or heat, drive smoothly with gradual stops and turns, and keep the radio at low volume or off entirely.

For longer trips (over 2 hours), plan rest stops to check on your guinea pigs and offer small amounts of water if they seem interested. Bring extra bedding and supplies in case of accidents, and have emergency veterinarian contact information for your destination area.

Your guinea pigs might make nervous sounds, huddle together for comfort, or eliminate more frequently due to stress. All of these responses are normal during transport.

4.4 The First Two Weeks: Adjustment and Trust Building

The first two weeks are crucial for your guinea pigs' successful transition to their new home. This period requires patience, consistency, and understanding rather than enthusiastic interaction attempts.

Days 1-3: Arrival and Settling In

Your guinea pigs' perspective: Everything is new and potentially scary! They need time to figure out that their new environment is safe and that you're a friend, not a threat.

QUICK TIP
Give your guinea pig a few days of quiet in their cage so they can feel safe before you start handling them.

What you should do: Provide quiet, consistent care by giving fresh food, water, and hay without trying to handle them yet. Speak softly when you're near their habitat so they learn to recognize your voice. Let them hide as much as they want—hiding is how guinea pigs cope with stress.

Normal first-day behaviors include lots of hiding (they might not come out for 12-24 hours), limited eating due to stress, restless exploration as they check out their new territory, and increased vocalizations as they call to each other for reassurance.

When to worry: If guinea pigs don't drink water after 24 hours, refuse all food for more than 36 hours, show obvious breathing difficulty, or seem injured, contact your veterinarian for guidance.

Days 4-7: Routine Development

Things start improving: Your

guinea pigs begin moving around more confidently, establish feeding patterns and favorite spots, and start showing curiosity about you instead of just fear.

Your role: Continue quiet, consistent care routines, use the same gentle voice during all interactions, and begin offering special treats through the habitat openings. Don't rush handling—let them approach you voluntarily.

Good signs: Guinea pigs eating normally, using all areas of their habitat comfortably, and making normal guinea pig sounds like soft purring or conversational squeaking with each other.

Days 8-14: Building Trust

When your guinea pigs are ready: They approach the front of their habitat when you appear, eat while you're nearby, and show relaxed body language instead of constant alertness for danger.

Start gentle interactions: Offer favorite vegetables from your flat palm, speak softly and consistently during care routines, and try very brief, gentle touches if guinea pigs seem receptive.

Take it slow: Some guinea pigs build trust quickly while others need weeks or even months. Follow their lead rather than forcing interaction on your timeline.

Signs of Successful Adjustment

By the end of two weeks, successfully adjusting guinea pigs eat and drink normally, use their entire habitat confidently, show curiosity about their human family, and maintain normal relationships with their guinea pig companions.

Remember that every guinea pig adjusts at their own pace. Some are confident explorers within days, while others are naturally more cautious and need extra time to feel secure. The key is consistency, patience, and reading your individual guinea pigs' signals rather than rushing the process.

> ▶ **Red flags that need attention:** Persistent eating problems, ongoing extreme fearfulness, health issues like continued breathing problems or digestive upset, or breakdown of the relationship between bonded pairs.

....

Coming up in Chapter 5: Learn to understand your guinea pigs' amazing communication system, from their famous wheeking calls to subtle body language that will help you build deeper relationships with these remarkably expressive animals.

Chapter 5: Understanding Your Guinea Pig

5.1 Reading Guinea Pig Body Language

Learning to understand what your guinea pigs are "saying" with their bodies is like cracking a secret code—and once you figure it out, you'll be amazed by how much they're actually communicating! Guinea pigs are incredibly expressive animals who tell you exactly how they're feeling if you know what to look for.

Happy Guinea Pig Signals

Relaxed and confident guinea pigs look comfortable and move naturally around their space. Their ears point forward with curiosity rather than flattening back with fear. They breathe quietly and steadily, and their fur lies smooth and normal against their bodies.

When guinea pigs feel good, they explore their habitat with obvious curiosity, sniffing around with their whiskers forward and moving with steady, confident steps. They'll use all parts of their home comfortably and engage in regular grooming sessions—guinea pigs only groom themselves when they feel completely safe.

The ultimate trust signal? When your guinea pigs feel secure enough to eat while you're nearby. This shows they consider you part of their safe environment rather than a potential threat.

Stress and Fear Signals

Scared guinea pigs look very different from confident ones. Their ears flatten back against their heads, their fur might puff up to make them look bigger, and they crouch low to the ground as if ready to run and hide at any moment.

QUICK TIP
Listen for different sounds. A happy guinea pig may purr, while a loud squeak usually means they want attention.

Stress behaviors include hiding excessively (refusing to come out even for favorite foods), pacing or repetitive movements, freezing completely when you approach, or focusing obsessively on grooming one area until the fur gets thin.

When guinea pigs are really frightened, they might breathe rapidly through their mouths, tremble visibly, or make distress sounds like squealing or alarm calls. Some guinea pigs will even empty their bladders suddenly when startled—it's a normal fear response, not a bathroom accident.

Pain and Illness Clues

Guinea pigs are masters at hiding when they don't feel well, but there are clues you can watch for.

Sick guinea pigs often sit in a hunched position with their backs rounded, move reluctantly or stay in one spot for long periods, and might grind their teeth (which indicates pain, not happiness like in some animals).

Other illness signals include changes in normal grooming habits, unusual breathing patterns, or being less social with their guinea pig companions and human family.

5.2 The Guinea Pig Sound Dictionary

Get ready for some serious entertainment! Guinea pigs are among the most talkative pets you can have, with a whole vocabulary of sounds that mean specific things. Learning their "language" helps you understand what they need and want.

Wheeking: The Famous Guinea Pig Call

The classic "wheek wheek wheek" is probably the sound that made you fall in love with guinea pigs in the first place! It's loud, demanding, and absolutely impossible to ignore—which is exactly the point.

Guinea pigs wheek when they hear the refrigerator door (they know where the good vegetables live!), see their favorite people enter the room, think it might be dinner time, or just want attention. It's basically their way of saying "Hey! I'm here and I want something!"

Some guinea pigs become professional wheekers who train their families to respond to every sound. While it's cute, you don't have to answer every wheek with food—sometimes they're just saying hello!

Purring: The Happy Sound

Unlike cat purring, guinea pig purring comes in different varieties. **Deep, rumbly purring** means your guinea pig is completely content and relaxed. You'll often hear this during gentle petting or when they're snuggled up comfortably.

Short, soft purring shows pleasure and satisfaction, especially during grooming or while eating favorite foods. It's like their way of saying "this feels good" or "this tastes amazing."

Popcorning: Pure Joy in Motion

This isn't a sound, but it's communication you'll definitely notice! **Popcorning** is when guinea pigs suddenly jump straight up in the air, often twisting or kicking their legs while airborne. It looks exactly like popcorn popping—hence the name.

Guinea pigs popcorn when they're feeling absolutely wonderful. You might see it during floor time, when they get special treats, during play with their companions, or sometimes just because they feel fantastic. It's one of the most delightful behaviors you'll ever witness, and it means you're doing something very right!

Other Important Guinea Pig Sounds

Chattering and "conversations" between guinea pigs sound like they're having detailed discussions about important guinea pig topics. These soft, rapid sounds help them stay connected and coordinate their activities.

Teeth chattering (different from conversational chattering) is a warning sound that means "back off" or "I'm not comfortable." It sounds sharper and more aggressive than friendly chattering.

Squealing or screaming indicates distress, fear, or pain and should always get your immediate attention to figure out what's wrong.

5.3 Daily Life and Natural Behaviors

Understanding when your guinea pigs are naturally active and what they like to do helps you work with their schedules instead of against them.

Guinea Pig Daily Rhythms

Guinea pigs are most active during early morning and evening hours—which means they're actually awake when you are! This makes them much more interactive pets than nocturnal animals who sleep while you're trying to play with them.

A typical guinea pig day includes waking up around 6-8 AM for breakfast and territory checking, resting during the middle of the day (but not deep sleep like hamsters), becoming more active around 3-6 PM, and having their most energetic period from 6-9 PM when they're ready for dinner and social time.

This schedule works great for families because guinea pigs are alert and social during after-school and evening hours when you have time to interact with them.

Eating All Day Long

Unlike animals that eat big meals at specific times, **guinea pigs are grazers** who nibble constantly throughout their active periods. This means they should always have hay available, and you'll often see them eating whenever you look at them.

QUICK TIP
Guinea pigs are most active in the morning and evening.

Guinea pigs are also very social eaters who enjoy meals together, take turns at food sources, and sometimes share particularly delicious items. Watching bonded pairs coordinate their eating is like watching a polite dinner conversation.

Social Behaviors That Strengthen Friendships

Mutual grooming between guinea pig pairs is one of the sweetest behaviors you'll observe. They focus on cleaning each other's ears, faces, and hard-to-reach areas while making soft, contented sounds.

Sleeping together in adorable guinea pig pile-ups provides warmth, security, and emotional comfort. Even guinea pigs who have separate territories during active periods often choose to rest together.

Coordinated activities show how bonded guinea pigs influence each other's decisions about when to eat, explore, or rest. It's like they have their own little social schedule that they follow together.

5.4 How Guinea Pigs Communicate with You

Once your guinea pigs settle into their new home, they'll start developing individual relationships with their human family members. Each guinea pig has their own communication style and personality.

Signs Your Guinea Pig Recognizes You

Excited greetings when you enter the room show that your guinea pig has learned you're someone special. They might wheek enthusiastically, approach the front of their habitat, or seem generally more alert and interested when you appear.

Calm acceptance during routine care activities like cleaning, feeding, and gentle handling indicates growing trust. Guinea pigs who trust their families remain relaxed rather than stressed during these necessary interactions.

Food sharing represents serious trust—when guinea pigs are willing to eat while you're nearby, accept hand-fed treats, or show excitement rather than fear when you handle their food sources.

Understanding What Your Guinea Pig Wants

Attention-seeking behaviors include persistent wheeking when they see you, standing against habitat walls, or engaging in amusing antics that seem designed to get your focus.

Request signals develop over time as guinea pigs learn to communicate specific wants. They might wheek in particular ways for favorite treats, stand in certain locations when they want floor time, or position themselves to indicate readiness for gentle handling.

Problem reporting happens when observant guinea pigs increase vocalizations or change behaviors to let you know something needs attention—like empty water bottles, soiled areas, or minor discomfort.

FUN FACT
Guinea pigs can have more than 20 different sounds to express how they feel, from happy chirps to curious wheeks!

Building Your Communication Relationship

When your guinea pig seems happy and engaged, continue what you're doing! Provide gentle positive reinforcement through calm voice and consistent care, and maintain routines that support their contentment.

When your guinea pig shows stress, reduce environmental stimulation, give them space to retreat, and evaluate their environment for possible problems or health concerns.

When your guinea pig appears to be asking for something, check their basic needs first (food, water, cleanliness), consider timing for natural activities like floor time, and respond consistently to reasonable requests while maintaining appropriate boundaries.

Learning your guinea pigs' unique communication styles creates genuine relationships rather than just caretaking arrangements. Each guinea pig develops individual ways of "talking" to their family, and understanding these personal languages strengthens your bond while helping you provide better care.

••••••••••••••••••••••••••••••••

Coming up in Chapter 6: Learn everything about guinea pig nutrition, from their critical Vitamin C requirements to building the perfect daily fresh food menu that keeps your guinea pigs healthy and happy throughout their lives.

Chapter 6: Feeding Your Guinea Pigs Right

6.1 Guinea Pig Nutrition Made Simple

Here's something amazing about guinea pigs: they're one of the few animals on Earth (besides humans!) who can't make their own Vitamin C. This makes their nutrition both more interesting and more important than other small pets. But don't worry—once you understand what guinea pigs need, providing excellent nutrition becomes as easy as any other daily routine.

Think of guinea pig nutrition like building the perfect meal plan for very small, very opinionated vegetarians who happen to have some unique dietary requirements!

What Makes Guinea Pig Nutrition Special

Guinea pigs evolved as grazers who spent most of their time munching on grasses and plants in the mountains of South America. This means they need constant access to hay (their favorite food!), daily fresh vegetables for essential vitamins, appropriate pellets for concentrated nutrition, and fresh water available at all times.

The Vitamin C difference is what makes guinea pig care unique. While your dog or cat can make Vitamin C in their bodies, guinea pigs must get it from their food every single day. Miss too many days, and they can get seriously sick. The good news? Providing enough Vitamin C is actually pretty easy once you know which foods are vitamin powerhouses!

Why this matters for your guinea pigs: Proper nutrition isn't just about preventing illness—it's about giving your guinea pigs energy for popcorning, shiny coats that feel amazing to pet, strong immune systems that keep them healthy, and long, happy lives filled with enthusiasm for meals and activities.

QUICK TIP
Offer fresh hay at all times. It keeps guinea pigs' teeth healthy and helps their digestion.

Understanding What Guinea Pigs Eat in the Wild vs. Home

In their natural habitat, guinea pigs spend most of their waking hours grazing on a variety of grasses, herbs, and occasional fruits or vegetables. Their wild diet consists of primarily fresh grasses and hay (80-90% of diet), diverse herbs and leafy plants, occasional fruits and vegetables, and very small amounts of seeds or grains.

The key difference between wild and home diets is variety and activity level. Wild guinea pigs might sample dozens of different plant types in a single day while burning tremendous energy through constant foraging. Pet guinea pigs need us to provide appropriate variety within a controlled framework that matches their less active lifestyle.

6.2 Hay: The Foundation of Everything

If guinea pigs could choose only one food to eat forever, they'd probably choose hay! It's their natural favorite and should make up about 80% of their daily diet.

FUN FACT
Guinea pigs eat their food twice! They produce special soft droppings called caecotropes that they eat again to absorb extra nutrients.

Why Guinea Pigs Love and Need Hay

Hay keeps their teeth healthy because guinea pig teeth grow continuously throughout their lives. The natural grinding action of chewing hay keeps teeth properly worn down and prevents painful overgrowth that can make eating impossible.

Hay provides the fiber their digestive systems need to work properly. Guinea pigs have complex digestive systems designed specifically for processing lots of high-fiber plant material, just like their wild ancestors.

Hay is mentally satisfying because it mimics their natural grazing behaviors. Eating hay gives guinea pigs something to do throughout the day, prevents boredom, and provides the psychological comfort of following natural instincts.

Timothy Hay for Daily Life

Timothy hay should be available 24/7 for adult guinea pigs. They'll nibble it constantly throughout their active periods, and that's exactly what they should be doing! You'll often see guinea pigs eating hay while doing other activities—it's like their version of snacking.

How much hay to expect: Guinea

pigs eat approximately their body weight in hay daily—which sounds like a lot but is completely normal! You'll go through hay faster than you might expect, and that's a good sign that your guinea pigs are eating properly.

FUN FACT
Guinea pigs can munch on hay for up to 6 hours a day. It's their favorite food and the key to keeping them healthy!

What good timothy hay looks like: Fresh, green color (not brown or yellow), sweet, pleasant smell (never musty or moldy), soft enough to be appealing but with some structure for dental benefits, and free from excessive dust or mold.

Different cuts of timothy hay: First cut has coarser stems and higher fiber (great for dental health), second cut has softer leaves and is more palatable (good for picky eaters), and third cut is very soft and leafy (like dessert hay for special occasions).

Special Hay Considerations

Young guinea pigs (under 6 months) benefit from alfalfa hay mixed with timothy hay because they need extra calcium and protein for rapid growth. The richer nutrition in alfalfa supports healthy development during this crucial period.

Pregnant and nursing mothers also need alfalfa hay's higher calcium and protein content to support pregnancy and milk production for babies.

Adult guinea pigs should stick primarily to timothy hay, with other varieties (orchard grass, meadow hay, oat hay) offered occasionally for variety and enrichment.

Hay storage and freshness: Store hay in cool, dry places with good air circulation, check regularly for mold or pest contamination, and use older hay first to maintain freshness. Bad hay can make guinea pigs sick, so quality matters!

6.3 The Magic of Vitamin C

Since guinea pigs can't make their own Vitamin C, they depend on you to provide it every day through their diet. Think of yourself as their personal nutrition specialist!

Daily Vitamin C Requirements

Adult guinea pigs need 30mg of Vitamin C daily—about the amount in one small red bell pepper. **Pregnant or nursing mothers need 100mg daily** to support pregnancy and milk production. **Growing guinea pigs need 50mg daily** to support healthy development.

Signs your guinea pigs are getting enough Vitamin C: They have energy for normal activities like exploring and playing, maintain healthy, glossy coats that feel soft, heal quickly from minor scratches or injuries, show enthusiasm for meals and new foods, and maintain good muscle tone and mobility.

Understanding Vitamin C Deficiency (Scurvy)

Early warning signs that guinea pigs aren't getting enough Vitamin C include decreased appetite and enthusiasm for food, slight lethargy or reduced activity levels, minor dental problems or reluctance to chew hard foods, and small changes in coat quality or grooming habits.

More serious symptoms include swollen, painful joints that affect movement, obvious dental problems like loose teeth, poor wound healing and increased injury susceptibility, and severe lethargy that interferes with normal activities.

The good news: Vitamin C deficiency is completely preventable with proper daily nutrition, and early stages can be quickly reversed with improved diet and veterinary guidance if needed.

Vitamin C Superstar Foods

Red bell peppers are absolutely magical for guinea pigs! One-quarter of a large red pepper provides more than enough daily Vitamin C (about 95mg), most guinea pigs think they taste like candy, they're crunchy and fun to eat, and they come in different colors (red, yellow, orange) for variety. Red peppers actually contain more Vitamin C than green ones!

Leafy green champions include fresh parsley (about 80mg per cup—most guinea pigs go crazy for this!), cilantro (about 70mg per cup—some love it, others aren't fans), kale (80mg per cup but offer 2-3 times weekly due to calcium content), and mustard greens (70mg per cup with spicy flavor many guinea pigs enjoy).

Broccoli and relatives provide amazing nutrition when offered 2-3 times weekly. Broccoli florets contain about 80mg Vitamin C per cup and are usually a big hit. Broccoli leaves (often thrown away by grocery stores) are actually higher in Vitamin C than the florets, and cauliflower leaves are another vitamin-rich option.

Important facts about Vitamin C: It breaks down rapidly when exposed to air, light, and heat, so fresh vegetables provide the most reliable source. Fortified pellets lose Vitamin C potency within 90 days of manufacturing, making fresh food your best strategy. Cooking destroys Vitamin C, so vegetables must be offered fresh and raw.

6.4 Building the Perfect Daily Veggie Salad

Get ready for one of the most fun parts of guinea pig ownership—creating delicious, healthy "salads" that will make your guinea pigs wheek with excitement every single day! Fresh vegetables aren't just treats for guinea pigs; they're essential daily nutrition that provides crucial Vitamin C, mental stimulation, and variety that makes mealtime the highlight of their day.

Daily Fresh Food Requirements

Every guinea pig needs about 1 cup of fresh vegetables daily—that's like a small salad made just for them. For pairs, you'll be preparing about 2 cups of fresh food every day, which sounds like a lot but becomes a quick, enjoyable routine.

QUICK TIP
Wash veggies before serving to remove dirt and chemicals that could upset your guinea pig's tummy.

The daily salad should include: 1-2 vegetables that are packed with Vitamin C (like red bell peppers or leafy greens), 2-3 additional vegetables for variety and different nutrients, a mix of textures (crunchy, leafy, soft) to keep things interesting and support dental health, and a rainbow of colors because different colors often mean different vitamins and nutrients.

Why guinea pigs love fresh food: It tastes amazing compared to dry pellets and hay, provides mental stimulation through different flavors and textures, gives them something exciting to look forward to each day, and lets them express individual preferences and personalities through food choices.

Daily Salad Foundation Vegetables

Romaine lettuce is like the reliable best friend of guinea pig salads—most guinea pigs love it, it's available everywhere year-round, provides good hydration with decent nutrition, and it's affordable for daily feeding. Other excellent daily lettuce options include green leaf lettuce (soft and appealing to picky eaters), red leaf lettuce (pretty color with antioxidants), and Boston lettuce (very soft, good for senior guinea pigs).

Never, ever iceberg lettuce! It's mostly water with very little nutrition and can cause diarrhea. Stick with the darker, more nutritious lettuce varieties that actually provide health benefits.

Fresh herbs that add excitement: Small amounts of fresh herbs make guinea pig salads feel gourmet! Fresh parsley is usually the biggest hit and packed with Vitamin C. Cilantro adds interesting flavor variety that some guinea pigs absolutely love (though others act like you've offered them something terrible). Basil provides aromatic interest in tiny amounts, and dill offers completely different taste experiences.

Everyday crunchy favorites include cucumber (provides refreshing crunch and hydration, works especially well during hot weather), zucchini (offers mild flavor that appeals to most guinea pigs and interesting texture variety), and celery (remove strings for safety, provides satisfying crunch).

Bell peppers in all colors are the superstars of guinea pig nutrition. Red peppers provide the most Vitamin C (about 190mg per cup), yellow and orange peppers offer excellent nutrition with appealing sweetness, and even green peppers provide substantial Vitamin C (about 120mg per cup). Most guinea pigs consider bell peppers absolutely irresistible!

Preparation tip: Remove all seeds and white parts, cut into strips that are easy for guinea pigs to hold and eat, and offer about 1/4 to 1/2 of a large pepper daily for optimal nutrition.

Weekly Variety Vegetables

These vegetables provide excellent nutrition but should be offered 2-3 times weekly rather than daily, because they're very rich in certain minerals and because they can cause digestive upset if overfed.

> **FUN FACT**
> *Guinea pigs have tiny taste buds that can tell sweet, sour, salty, and bitter foods apart. Most of them love sweet veggies the most!*

Higher calcium powerhouses: Kale, collard greens, and turnip greens are incredible nutrition sources, but they're also high in calcium. While calcium is important for guinea pig health, too much can contribute to urinary problems in some guinea pigs. Offer these nutrient-dense greens 2-3 times weekly for maximum benefit without overdoing mineral content.

Cruciferous vegetables that can cause gas: Broccoli, cauliflower, cabbage, and Brussels sprouts provide excellent nutrition but can cause digestive upset if fed too frequently. Offer small amounts 2-3 times weekly and watch for any signs of bloating or discomfort.

Root vegetables for special occasions: Carrots are like candy to many guinea pigs—sweet, crunchy, and absolutely irresistible. However, their natural sugar content means they should be offered as special treats rather than daily staples. Give 1-2 baby carrots or thin slices 2-3 times weekly.

Sweet potato (always raw, never cooked!) provides different nutrients and appealing sweetness. Offer small cubes occasionally for variety, but monitor for any digestive changes.

Beets are interesting options that some guinea pigs love. Just don't be alarmed if their urine turns pink afterward—it's completely normal and harmless!

FUN FACT
Guinea pigs eat small meals all day long. Their tummies work best when they are constantly nibbling.

Safe Daily Additions

Cherry tomatoes (always remove green parts completely) provide Vitamin C and appealing sweetness, but offer in moderation due to natural sugars and acidity.

Other safe daily options include small amounts of safe herbs for variety, occasional additions of other approved vegetables, and seasonal options when available and affordable.

6.5 Fruits: Nature's Guinea Pig Desserts

Fruits should be thought of as desserts in guinea pig nutrition—delicious, enjoyed in small amounts, and offered occasionally rather than regularly. The high sugar content in fruits can cause digestive upset, dental problems, and weight gain if overfed, but appropriate amounts provide enrichment and variety.

Berry Treats That Guinea Pigs Love

Strawberries, blueberries, raspberries, and blackberries make excellent occasional treats that most guinea pigs find absolutely irresistible. Offer 1/2 to 1 small strawberry or 3-5 blueberries twice weekly. Always remove any green parts or stems before serving.

Most guinea pigs go absolutely crazy for berries, making them excellent options for training treats, bonding activities, or special rewards during handling and grooming sessions.

Other Safe Fruit Options

Apple and pear (always remove seeds which can be harmful!) can be offered as thin slices twice weekly. Choose sweet varieties that appeal to guinea pig preferences, and always cut pieces small enough to prevent choking.

Grapes (cut in half to prevent choking) work as occasional treats, though some guinea pig experts recommend avoiding them due to potential kidney concerns in small animals.

Melon varieties like cantaloupe and honeydew provide hydration and sweetness in small amounts during hot weather.

Small orange segments provide excellent Vitamin C but are quite acidic, so offer very sparingly to prevent mouth irritation.

Fruit Safety Guidelines

Portion control is crucial: Total fruit per guinea pig should never exceed 1-2 tablespoons twice weekly. Pieces should be small enough to prevent choking but large enough that guinea pigs can hold and eat them easily.

Frequency matters: Never offer fruit daily, and ideally limit to 2-3 times per week maximum. Some guinea pigs handle fruit better than others, so watch for individual tolerance.

Signs of fruit overconsumption include soft stools or diarrhea, decreased interest in hay and pellets (choosing sweet fruit over nutritious foods), gradual weight gain over time, and increased thirst or changes in urination patterns.

Fruits to Avoid Completely

Dangerous fruits that can harm guinea pigs: Rhubarb contains toxic compounds that can cause serious illness. Avocado (all parts) contains persin which is toxic to small animals. Dried fruits are too concentrated in sugars and often contain harmful preservatives.

Problematic options: Bananas are extremely high in sugar and can cause serious digestive upset even in tiny amounts. Canned fruits usually contain added sugars and preservatives that are harmful to guinea pigs.

6.6 Pellets: Concentrated Nutrition Done Right

High-quality pellets provide concentrated nutrition that supplements hay and fresh vegetables, but they should never be the primary component of your guinea pig's diet. Think of them as vitamin-packed supplements rather than main meals.

Choosing Quality Guinea Pig Pellets

Essential pellet characteristics: Look for pellets that list timothy hay as the first ingredient to ensure they match your guinea pig's primary dietary needs. Choose plain, uniform pellets without colorful bits, nuts, seeds, or dried fruits mixed in, as these allow selective eating where guinea pigs pick favorite parts and ignore nutritious components.

Quality indicators include: Fortified with Vitamin C (minimum 20mg per serving, though fresh vegetables remain your primary source), appropriate protein levels (14-16% for adults, 16-18% for pregnant/nursing females), fresh dating within 6 months of manufacture for optimal nutrition, and natural preservatives rather than artificial chemicals.

Avoid pellet mixes with nuts, seeds, colorful pieces, or dried fruits. These "gourmet" mixes often encourage selective eating and may contain items that are too high in fat or sugar for regular guinea pig consumption.

Proper Pellet Portions and Timing

Adult guinea pigs need about 1/4 cup of pellets daily—that's a smaller amount than many people expect! Measuring portions rather than free-feeding prevents obesity and ensures your guinea pigs eat their hay and vegetables enthusiastically.

FUN FACT
Guinea pigs' teeth grow about 2 millimeters each week, so constant chewing on hay keeps them trimmed and healthy.

Special portion considerations: Young guinea pigs (under 6 months) can have 1/2 cup daily while they're growing rapidly. Pregnant females need 1/2 cup daily during pregnancy and nursing to support increased nutritional demands. Senior guinea pigs may need adjusted portions based on weight and activity levels.

Feeding timing strategies: Most families feed pellets during evening hours when guinea pigs are naturally most active and hungry. You can divide the daily portion into morning and evening meals if preferred, or provide the full amount during peak activity periods.

Pellet Storage and Freshness

Maintaining pellet quality: Store pellets in airtight containers in cool, dry locations away from direct sunlight. Use pellets within 6 months of purchase for optimal nutrition, especially for Vitamin C content. Check regularly for signs of insect contamination, mold, or rancid odors that indicate spoilage.

Signs of spoiled pellets include: Rancid or unusual odors that differ from the normal grain smell, visible mold or discoloration anywhere on pellets, insect infestation or larvae, and crumbly texture that indicates age and nutrient loss.

6.7 Water: The Often-Forgotten Essential

Fresh, clean water should be available 24/7, and guinea pigs drink more than you might expect—especially when they're eating lots of hay and dry pellets. Proper hydration supports everything from digestion to temperature regulation.

Water Delivery Systems That Work

FUN FACT
Guinea pigs use their whiskers to explore food and feel around their bowl, helping them find tasty bites even in the dark.

Water bottles work well for most guinea pig setups because they keep water clean and free from bedding contamination, allow easy monitoring of consumption levels, prevent spills that could dampen bedding and create mold problems, and can accommodate multiple bottles for backup systems.

Choose appropriate bottle sizes: 16-32 ounce bottles work well for guinea pig pairs, with wide mouth openings for easy cleaning and filling. Quality ball bearing mechanisms prevent leaking while ensuring proper water flow, and secure mounting systems must withstand guinea pig manipulation.

Water bowls provide more natural drinking positions for guinea pigs and work well for animals who prefer open water sources. Use heavy ceramic construction that prevents tipping and moving, wide shallow designs for easy access, and smooth interiors that clean easily and prevent bacterial buildup.

Many families use both bottles and bowls to provide options, ensure backup water availability if one source fails, and accommodate individual drinking preferences between guinea pigs.

Monitoring Water Consumption

Normal water intake: Adult guinea pigs typically drink 100-300ml per day depending on diet, weather, and individual activity levels. Fresh vegetable consumption reduces water bottle usage since vegetables provide hydration. Hot weather or dry diets increase water requirements significantly.

Signs of adequate hydration include bright, clear eyes without sunken appearance, moist mucous membranes in mouth and nose, elastic skin that snaps back quickly when gently pinched, regular urination with pale yellow color, and normal energy levels with good appetite.

Dehydration warning signs include sunken eyes or dry mucous membranes, skin that remains tented when gently pinched, dark yellow or significantly reduced urination, lethargy or decreased appetite, and dry, sticky mouth.

6.8 Dangerous Foods: What to Avoid Completely

Understanding which foods can harm your guinea pig is just as important as knowing what to feed them. Guinea pigs have sensitive digestive systems, and some foods that are healthy for humans can be toxic or dangerous for these small animals.

Foods That Cause Digestive Problems

Items that cause bloating, gas, or diarrhea: Iceberg lettuce has high water content and low nutrition that can cause diarrhea and provides little health benefit. Beans and legumes (raw or cooked) cause severe digestive upset and bloating. Corn is difficult to digest and can cause intestinal blockages.

Dairy products including milk, cheese, and yogurt cannot be digested properly by guinea pigs after weaning, causing severe diarrhea and dehydration.

Processed human foods containing preservatives, artificial colors, or excess sodium can cause various health problems and should never be offered.

Foods That Can Cause Urinary Problems

Very high-calcium foods like spinach can contribute to urinary sludge and bladder stone formation when fed regularly. Beet greens and Swiss chard are also very high in oxalates and should be limited.

Signs of urinary problems include straining to urinate, blood in urine (pink or red coloration), white gritty deposits in urine, and signs of pain during urination.

> ### Toxic Foods That Can Be Fatal ☠️
>
> **Foods that can cause serious illness or death:** Chocolate contains theobromine and caffeine, both toxic to guinea pigs even in small amounts. Onions and garlic contain compounds that damage red blood cells, leading to serious anemia. Rhubarb leaves and stems contain high levels of oxalic acid that cause kidney problems and can be fatal.
>
> **Avocado (all parts)** contains persin, a compound that causes heart and respiratory problems in small animals. Even tiny amounts can be dangerous.
>
> **Raw beans and potatoes** contain natural toxins that cause severe digestive upset and can be life-threatening. Green potatoes are particularly dangerous due to solanine content.
>
> **Human foods that are dangerous:** Caffeinated beverages (coffee, tea, sodas) contain stimulants that can cause heart problems in small animals. Alcoholic beverages are extremely toxic and can cause organ damage even in tiny amounts. Sugary treats like candy, cookies, and cake contain harmful artificial ingredients and dangerous sugar levels.

Plants and Household Items That Are Dangerous

Common houseplants that are toxic include all lily varieties (extremely toxic), azaleas and rhododendrons (cause heart problems), poinsettias (cause mouth irritation), ivy varieties (cause digestive and respiratory problems), and oleander (extremely toxic to all animals).

Outdoor plants to avoid include wild onions and garlic, foxglove (affects heart function), buttercups (cause mouth irritation), and oak leaves and acorns (tannins cause digestive upset).

Emergency Response to Suspected Poisoning

Immediate steps if you suspect poisoning: Remove your guinea pig from the source immediately and don't induce vomiting (guinea pigs cannot vomit). Contact your veterinarian or emergency clinic immediately and save samples of the suspected poison for identification.

Information to provide to veterinarian: What was consumed and approximate amount, when the exposure occurred, current symptoms or behavior changes, your guinea pig's weight and age, and any current health problems.

6.9 Special Dietary Considerations

Different life stages and health conditions require modifications to standard guinea pig nutrition. Understanding these special needs helps ensure optimal health throughout your guinea pigs' 6-8 year lifespans.

Growing Guinea Pigs (Under 6 Months)

Increased nutritional needs: Young guinea pigs require higher protein (18-20% compared to 16-18% for adults), unlimited pellet access rather than measured portions, alfalfa hay mixed with timothy hay for extra calcium and protein, and extra Vitamin C (50mg daily) to support rapid growth.

Growth monitoring: Weigh young guinea pigs weekly to ensure steady weight gain, watch for proper development of teeth and body condition, adjust portions if growth seems too rapid or too slow, and transition gradually to adult portions around 6 months of age.

Pregnant and Nursing Guinea Pigs

Dramatically increased needs: Pregnant and nursing females need 18-20% protein throughout gestation and lactation, unlimited food access with no portion restrictions, alfalfa hay provided freely throughout pregnancy and nursing, and double Vitamin C requirements (100mg daily).

Special support: Provide constant access to high-quality food since pregnant mothers cannot go long periods without eating, offer energy-dense foods and extra calcium sources, and work with veterinarian for monitoring throughout pregnancy and lactation.

Senior Guinea Pigs (4+ Years)

Age-related adjustments: Provide softer foods if dental problems develop, focus on easily digestible vegetables, offer frequent small meals rather than large portions, and monitor weight carefully to prevent both obesity and unwanted weight loss.

Addressing age-related challenges: Soften pellets with water if needed, offer softer vegetables and avoid very hard foods, place food sources closer together for easier access, and work with veterinarian to manage any chronic health conditions.

• •

Coming up in Chapter 7: Learn safe handling techniques for larger pets, discover bonding activities that work with guinea pig social nature, and explore training and enrichment that strengthens your relationship while keeping everyone safe and happy.

Chapter 7: Handling and Bonding

7.1 Safe Handling

Learning to handle guinea pigs safely is like learning to hold a small, warm, living teddy bear that happens to have opinions and preferences! Guinea pigs are much bigger than hamsters, which makes them easier to hold securely, but they're also more delicate than their sturdy appearance suggests.

The great news is that guinea pigs' social nature makes them wonderful pets for gentle handling once you understand their needs. Unlike animals who prefer to avoid human contact, most guinea pigs can learn to genuinely enjoy spending time with their families.

Understanding Guinea Pig Bodies

Guinea pigs need different support than smaller pets because they're heavier (1-3 pounds!) and longer. Think of supporting them like holding a small loaf of bread—you need both hands to keep everything secure and comfortable.

What makes guinea pigs different: Their spines can be hurt if you don't support their bodies properly, they have strong back legs that can kick if they feel insecure, and they're naturally nervous about being lifted from above (which feels like a predator attack to them).

Reading guinea pig readiness: Guinea pigs ready for handling look alert but relaxed, approach the front of their habitat when you're nearby, and show calm body language with normal breathing and comfortable postures.

The Two-Handed Approach

Always use both hands when lifting guinea pigs. Place one hand under their chest area supporting their front legs, while your other hand supports their hindquarters and back legs. Lift smoothly and keep them close to your body so they feel secure.

FUN FACT

Guinea pigs remember gentle handling. With patience, they can learn to relax in your arms and may even start to purr when cuddled.

Never grab from above or lift by front legs only—this terrifies guinea pigs and can cause injuries. Instead, let them see your hands coming and give them a chance to sniff and investigate before lifting.

Signs you're doing it right: Your guinea pig feels secure and supported, remains calm during lifting, and settles comfortably once held. If they struggle frantically or seem panicked, put them down gently and try again later.

Building Trust with Naturally Social Animals

Guinea pigs are social creatures who want to be part of a family—they just need to learn that you're a safe, trustworthy member of their group.

Start with treats and gentle voices during daily care routines. Offer favorite vegetables through habitat openings while speaking softly, so guinea pigs learn to associate your presence with good things happening.

Let them approach you rather than forcing interaction. Curious guinea pigs will often come to investigate your hands, especially if you smell like interesting vegetables!

Respect their boundaries when they indicate they need space. Guinea pigs who feel their signals are respected are much more likely to choose interaction voluntarily in the future.

7.2 Lap Time: The Ultimate Guinea Pig Experience

Once your guinea pigs trust you, lap time becomes one of the most rewarding parts of guinea pig ownership. Many guinea pigs genuinely enjoy snuggling with their families while watching TV or just relaxing together.

Setting Up for Lap Time Success

Choose comfortable seating where you can sit still for 15-30 minutes without needing to move around.

Use a soft towel on your lap to absorb any accidents (guinea pigs sometimes urinate when relaxed) and provide texture they can grip with their feet.

Start with short sessions of 5-10 minutes and gradually increase time as your guinea pig becomes more comfortable.

Keep the environment calm with quiet household activity and minimal sudden noises.

What Great Lap Time Looks Like

Relaxed guinea pigs settle comfortably against your body, may stretch out

or even close their eyes briefly, and make soft, contented sounds like gentle purring. Some guinea pigs love to explore your clothes, sniff your hands, or even groom themselves while being held.

Signs to end lap time: If guinea pigs become restless, try to hide in your clothes, or show stress signals like rapid breathing, it's time to return them gently to their habitat.

Individual preferences matter: Some guinea pigs become complete lap pets who could snuggle for hours, while others prefer shorter visits or more active interaction. Learn what each guinea pig enjoys most!

Making Lap Time Special

Include both guinea pigs in lap time sessions when possible—many pairs feel more comfortable together and enjoy shared snuggle time.

Use lap time for gentle bonding through soft talking, very gentle petting (if they enjoy it), and just peaceful companionship.

Make it routine by offering lap time during consistent times when your guinea pigs are naturally alert but calm, like early evening hours.

7.3 Floor Time: Exercise and Adventure

Guinea pigs need daily exercise outside their habitat, and floor time provides both physical activity and mental stimulation that keeps them healthy and happy.

Creating Safe Floor Time Areas

Guinea pig-proof a room by removing electrical cords, blocking access to small spaces where guinea pigs could get stuck, and ensuring no toxic plants or dangerous objects are accessible.

Create boundaries using exercise pens, furniture, or guinea pig-safe barriers to define the play area.

Provide multiple hiding spots throughout the space using cardboard boxes, tunnels, or familiar hideouts from their habitat.

Always supervise floor time—never leave guinea pigs unsupervised outside their secure habitat, even in guinea pig-proofed areas.

Making Floor Time Fun

Start with short sessions of 15-20 minutes and gradually increase as guinea pigs become comfortable exploring. **Include both guinea pigs** so they can support each other and play together during exploration.

QUICK TIP
Always support your guinea pig's bottom and chest when picking them up so they feel safe and secure.

Add enrichment like cardboard boxes to explore, tunnels to run through, safe climbing structures, and scattered treats for foraging fun.

Watch for guinea pig personalities to emerge during floor time—some are bold explorers, others prefer to stay close to familiar objects, and many become playful in ways you don't see in their habitat.

Floor Time Success Signs

Happy guinea pigs during floor time explore confidently, may popcorn with excitement, interact normally with their companions, and show curiosity about new objects and areas.

Time to go home: When guinea pigs seek hiding spots consistently, seem less interested in exploration, or start heading toward their habitat, they're ready to return home.

7.4 Simple Training and Enrichment

While guinea pigs aren't as trainable as dogs, they can learn simple responses and enjoy activities that challenge their minds and strengthen family bonds.

Basic Training That Works

Name recognition develops naturally through consistent use during positive interactions. Use your guinea pigs' names during feeding, gentle handling, and daily care so they learn to associate their names with good experiences.

Coming when called works for some guinea pigs, especially when motivated by favorite treats. Start by calling their names when they're already moving toward you, then reward with vegetables and praise.

Target training using your hand or a specific object helps guinea pigs learn to move to designated areas. This can be useful for encouraging them to enter carriers or move to specific spots during floor time.

Understanding Individual Learning Styles

Some guinea pigs are eager students who pick up routines quickly and seem to enjoy learning new things.

Others are more independent and prefer to do things their own way, which is perfectly normal and should be respected.

Success in guinea pig training is measured by positive interactions, reduced stress during necessary handling, and stronger bonds between guinea pigs and their families rather than complex trick performance.

> ### Enrichment That Engages Guinea Pig Minds
>
> **Foraging games** satisfy natural behaviors by hiding favorite vegetables around their habitat or play area.
>
> **Cardboard box exploration** provides temporary hideouts and chewing opportunities that guinea pigs find irresistible.
>
> **Puzzle feeding** using toilet paper tubes stuffed with hay or vegetables encourages problem-solving and extends eating time.
>
> **Rearranging habitat features** weekly provides new challenges and exploration opportunities.
>
> **Social enrichment** for pairs includes parallel activities during floor time, shared exploration of new objects, and opportunities to coordinate their activities naturally.

Building strong relationships with guinea pigs combines understanding their natural behaviors with respect for their individual personalities. The social nature of guinea pigs makes them wonderful companions for families who approach interaction with patience, consistency, and genuine appreciation for these remarkable animals.

The time invested in proper handling and trust-building creates bonds that enrich both guinea pig and human lives, providing years of rewarding companionship and mutual affection.

Coming up in Chapter 8 : Learn essential grooming skills including nail trimming, coat care for different breeds, and physical maintenance that keeps guinea pigs comfortable and healthy throughout their lives.

Chapter 8: Grooming and Physical Care

8.1 Making Grooming a Bonding Experience

Grooming your guinea pigs isn't just about keeping them looking beautiful—it's one of the best ways to strengthen your bond while keeping them healthy and comfortable! Unlike hamsters who handle most of their grooming independently, guinea pigs genuinely benefit from gentle human assistance and often learn to enjoy the attention.

Think of grooming as spa time for your guinea pigs, where you get to pamper them while checking that everything's healthy and happy. Many guinea pigs actually find gentle brushing and nail care relaxing once they get used to the routine.

Why Guinea Pigs Need Your Help

Guinea pigs have limited flexibility compared to cats or other pets, so they can't reach all areas of their bodies for thorough self-grooming. In the wild, guinea pigs groom each other, so domestic guinea pigs appreciate gentle human assistance with areas they can't manage alone.

Regular grooming lets you spot problems early like small cuts, skin irritation, or changes in coat condition that might indicate health issues. It's much easier to address minor problems before they become serious concerns.

Grooming time becomes quality bonding time when approached with patience and gentleness. Many guinea pigs learn to associate grooming with positive attention and may even purr contentedly during brushing sessions.

Grooming Supplies That Make Life Easier

Essential tools for all guinea pigs: A soft-bristled brush for regular grooming and debris removal, a fine-toothed metal comb for working through tangles, small scissors for trimming mats when necessary, nail clippers designed for small animals, and soft towels for wrapping nervous guinea pigs during grooming.

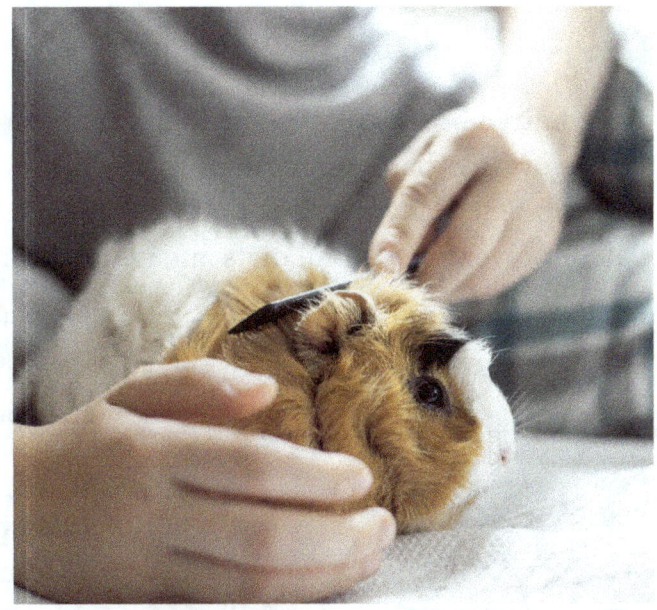

Nice-to-have supplies: A slicker brush for removing loose fur during shedding periods, detangling spray made specifically for guinea pigs, a grooming table or secure surface, and good lighting for thorough examination.

Creating positive grooming experiences: Start with very short sessions and gradually increase time, use treats and gentle praise throughout grooming, let guinea pigs see and sniff grooming tools before using them, and always stop if guinea pigs show serious stress signals.

8.2 Daily Brushing for Happy Guinea Pigs

Most guinea pigs benefit from some daily brushing, though the amount needed varies dramatically between short-haired and long-haired breeds.

Short-Haired Guinea Pig Grooming

Short-haired breeds (American, Abyssinian, Rex) need much less grooming than their long-haired cousins, but they still appreciate regular attention.

Quick daily routine: A few minutes of gentle brushing removes loose fur, distributes natural oils through their coat, provides bonding time, and lets you check for any skin problems or parasites.

What to watch for: Even short-haired guinea pigs can develop small mats behind their ears, under their legs, or around their hindquarters. Catching these early makes removal much easier and more comfortable.

Seasonal considerations: Short-haired guinea pigs may shed more during spring and fall, making daily brushing more important during these periods to prevent loose fur from creating mats.

> **QUICK TIP**
> *Brush long-haired guinea pigs often to prevent tangles and keep their coats clean.*

Long-Haired Guinea Pig Daily Care

Long-haired breeds (Peruvian, Silkie) are absolutely gorgeous but require much more grooming commitment. Daily care isn't optional—it's essential for preventing painful mats and maintaining their health.

Why daily brushing matters: Long guinea pig hair tangles easily, especially around areas where they eat, drink, and eliminate. Mats can become so tight they pull on skin and restrict movement, causing real discomfort.

Daily routine that works: Spend 10-15 minutes each day gently brushing through their entire coat, pay special attention to problem areas like hindquarters and under legs, work through small tangles immediately before they become serious mats, and keep hair around eating areas trimmed shorter for easier maintenance.

Making it manageable: Many families find that keeping long-haired guinea pigs in "pet cuts" (shorter overall length) reduces grooming time while maintaining coat health and guinea pig comfort.

Brushing Techniques That Work

Start gently with soft brush strokes in the direction of hair growth. Work systematically from head to tail, spending extra time on areas that mat easily.

For tangles, hold the hair above the tangle to prevent pulling on skin, work from the ends of the hair toward the roots, and use detangling spray sparingly if needed.

Watch guinea pig body language during brushing. Relaxed guinea pigs may close their eyes, make soft sounds, or even seem to fall asleep during gentle grooming.

8.3 Nail Trimming Made Simple

Guinea pig nails grow continuously and must be trimmed regularly to prevent overgrowth, injuries, and mobility problems. Learning to trim nails safely is one of the most important grooming skills for guinea pig families.

Why Nail Trims Are Essential

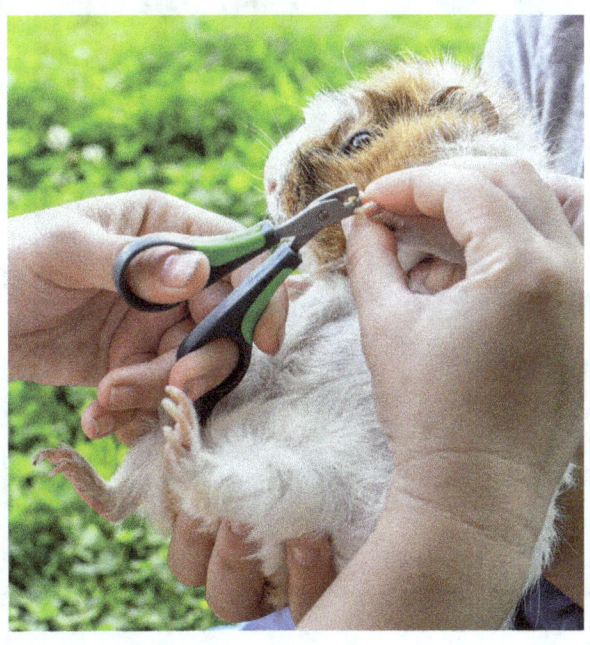

Overgrown nails cause real problems: They can curl and grow into foot pads (causing pain and infection), catch on bedding and toys (leading to torn nails), affect how guinea pigs walk and move, and make it harder for guinea pigs to groom themselves properly.

Most adult guinea pigs need nail trims every 4-6 weeks, though some grow nails faster than others. Young guinea pigs may need more frequent trims due to faster growth, while senior guinea pigs may need closer monitoring as they become less active.

Safe Nail Trimming Technique

Get prepared first: Use good lighting so you can see nail structure clearly, have styptic powder handy in case of minor accidents, and consider having a helper for guinea pigs who are nervous about nail trims.

The gentle approach: Wrap your guinea pig loosely in a soft towel, leaving one foot exposed at a time. Gently press on the foot pad to extend each nail, and look for the pink "quick" inside white nails.

QUICK TIP
Check your guinea pig's nails every few weeks. Keeping them trimmed prevents pain and helps them walk comfortably.

Safe cutting: Cut only the white portion of the nail, staying well away from the pink quick inside. Make quick, decisive cuts rather than slow crushing motions, and cut straight across rather than at angles.

For dark nails that make it hard to see the quick, use very bright light and cut very conservatively—it's better to trim small amounts frequently than risk cutting too much at once.

When Nail Trimming Goes Wrong

If you accidentally cut the quick (it happens to everyone eventually!), stay calm and apply styptic powder immediately to stop bleeding. Apply gentle pressure with a clean cloth if bleeding continues, and contact your veterinarian if bleeding doesn't stop or if you notice signs of infection later.

For guinea pigs who hate nail trims, try shorter sessions where you trim just a few nails at a time, use better restraint techniques to help them feel more secure, practice handling their feet during regular petting to build tolerance, or consider professional grooming for difficult cases.

8.4 Ear Care and Health Monitoring

Guinea pig ears usually stay pretty clean on their own, but regular gentle checking helps you spot problems early and maintain overall health.

Normal vs. Problem Ears

Healthy guinea pig ears look clean and dry inside, have pink skin without redness or swelling, don't have strong odors or unusual discharge, and don't cause guinea pigs to scratch excessively or shake their heads.

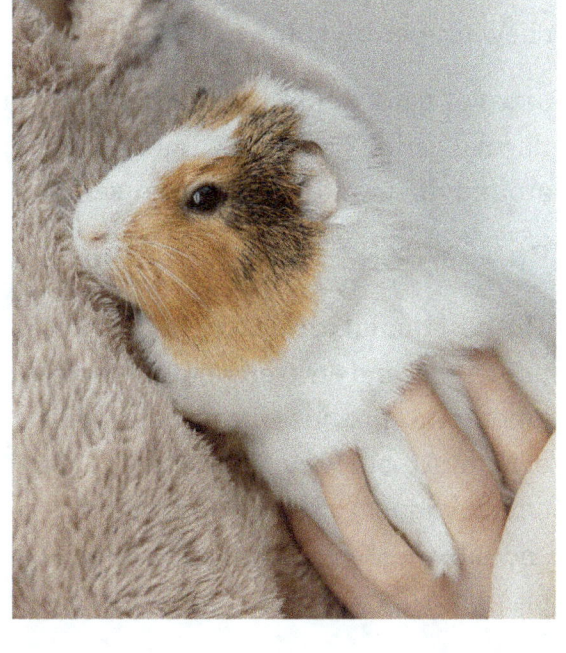

Signs that need veterinary attention include dark, smelly discharge, redness, swelling, or obvious irritation, excessive scratching at ears or frequent head shaking, balance problems or head tilting, and strong, unpleasant odors.

Safe Ear Cleaning

When light cleaning is appropriate: Remove visible debris or light wax buildup that appears dry and non-irritated. Use only cotton balls or soft cloths—never cotton swabs that could damage ear canals.

Simple cleaning technique: Hold your guinea pig securely, gently fold the ear flap to expose the interior, use a damp cotton ball to wipe only areas you can see clearly, and work from inside out to avoid pushing debris deeper.

When NOT to clean ears: If there are signs of infection (redness, swelling, discharge), if guinea pigs show pain when ears are touched, or if you notice unusual growths or changes. These situations need veterinary evaluation, not home cleaning.

8.5 Dental Health: Keeping Those Teeth in Shape

Guinea pig teeth grow continuously throughout their lives, making dental monitoring and care essential for preventing serious problems that can make eating difficult or impossible.

QUICK TIP
Look at your guinea pig's teeth regularly. Overgrown teeth can make eating hard and may need a vet's help.

Understanding Guinea Pig Teeth

Continuous growth means guinea pig teeth never stop growing, requiring constant natural wear through proper chewing. **Normal wear** happens when guinea pigs eat appropriate amounts of hay, chew proper toys, and grind their teeth naturally during eating.

Signs of good dental health include straight, even teeth without overgrowth, normal eating behavior without dropping food, no drooling or wetness around the mouth, and regular self-grooming without difficulty.

Supporting Natural Dental Health

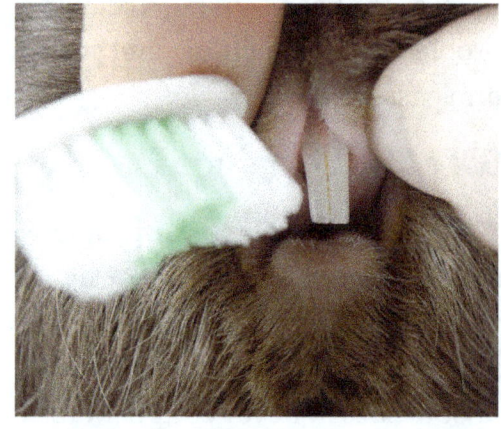

The best dental care happens through proper diet and environment. Unlimited timothy hay provides the primary source of natural tooth wear, appropriate pellets offer additional chewing opportunities, and safe wooden chew toys give guinea pigs extra options for natural grinding.

Environmental support includes providing varied textures in food and toys, offering fresh branches from safe fruit trees (apple, pear), and ensuring guinea pigs have constant access to appropriate chewing materials.

Recognizing Dental Problems

Warning signs that need veterinary attention include difficulty eating or dropping food frequently, visible overgrowth of front teeth, drooling or constant wetness around the mouth, weight loss despite good appetite, and reluctance to eat hay or other hard foods.

Emergency dental signs include complete inability to eat or drink, visible broken teeth with bleeding, severe drooling that prevents keeping the chin dry, and obvious signs of mouth pain like reluctance to be touched around the face.

Daily Dental Monitoring

Quick daily checks include observing normal eating behavior, watching for food dropping or difficulty chewing, checking that chin and chest stay dry, and listening for normal vs. excessive tooth grinding sounds.

Weekly detailed observation involves gently lifting lips to observe front teeth, checking for symmetry and proper alignment, looking for appropriate wear patterns, and noting any changes from previous observations.

8.6 When to Seek Professional Help

Sometimes grooming and physical care needs exceed what families can safely provide at home. Knowing when to seek professional help ensures your guinea pigs get appropriate care while preventing problems from becoming serious.

Professional Grooming Services

Consider professional grooming for: Severely matted long-haired guinea pigs that are beyond home care capabilities, aggressive guinea pigs who won't tolerate necessary grooming from family members, special occasions when perfect grooming is desired, or when family circumstances prevent adequate grooming time.

Finding guinea pig-experienced groomers: Ask your exotic pet veterinarian for referrals, contact local guinea pig rescue organizations for recommendations, interview groomers about their small animal experience, and visit facilities to ensure appropriate handling and safety practices.

Veterinary Grooming Needs

Nail trimming help: If family members can't safely trim nails, many veterinary clinics offer nail trimming services.

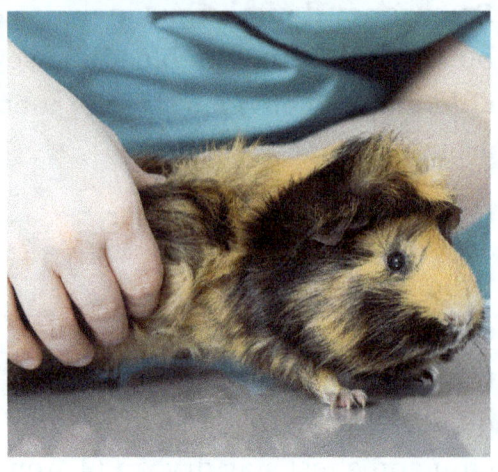

Dental problems: Overgrown teeth, dental abscesses, or eating difficulties require veterinary intervention. Never attempt to trim overgrown teeth at home—this requires professional equipment and expertise.

Skin and coat problems: Persistent mats, skin irritation, or suspected parasites need professional evaluation and treatment rather than home remedies.

Building Grooming Into Family Life

Making grooming sustainable: Choose routines that fit your family's schedule and abilities, assign age-appropriate grooming tasks to children with adult supervision, create positive associations with grooming through treats and praise, and establish backup plans for busy periods.

Teaching children proper grooming: Start with simple tasks like gentle brushing, always supervise nail trimming and more complex care, emphasize the importance of reading guinea pig signals, and celebrate successes to build confidence.

Regular grooming and physical care become enjoyable bonding experiences that strengthen relationships between guinea pigs and their families while maintaining health and comfort. The time invested in learning proper techniques pays dividends in easier care routines and stronger connections with these wonderful pets.

....

Coming up in Chapter 9: Learn to recognize signs of health and illness, understand common guinea pig health problems, and develop relationships with veterinary professionals who can support your guinea pigs' health throughout their 6-8 year lives.

Chapter 9: Keeping Your Guinea Pig Healthy

9.1 What Happy, Healthy Guinea Pigs Look Like

Learning to recognize when your guinea pigs are feeling great is one of the most important skills you'll develop as a guinea pig family! Healthy guinea pigs have obvious enthusiasm for life—they're active, curious, social, and genuinely fun to be around.

The best part about guinea pig health monitoring? Guinea pigs who feel good aren't shy about showing it! Healthy guinea pigs wheek with excitement, popcorn during play time, explore their environment confidently, and interact enthusiastically with their families.

Physical Signs of Great Health

Bright, clear eyes are like windows into guinea pig health. Healthy guinea pigs have alert, shiny eyes that follow movement and show interest in what's happening around them. Their eyes should be clear without any discharge, cloudiness, or excessive tearing.

Clean, appropriately moist noses from normal sniffing and investigating are perfect. Healthy guinea pig noses should be slightly damp but never runny or crusty. Guinea pigs use their noses constantly to explore their world, so some moisture is completely normal.

Gorgeous, glossy coats reflect excellent nutrition and overall well-being. Healthy guinea pig fur feels soft, lies smoothly against their bodies (except for naturally textured breeds), and has a natural shine that's obvious when they move around.

Good body condition means your guinea pigs maintain appropriate weight for their size and age. You should be able to feel their ribs gently but not see them prominently. Healthy guinea pigs move easily and comfortably without seeming stiff or reluctant to be active.

Quiet, regular breathing through their noses shows excellent respiratory health. You should rarely notice guinea pig breathing unless you're specifically watching them, and they should never seem to struggle or work hard to breathe.

Behavioral Signs of Guinea Pig Happiness

Enthusiastic eating is one of the best indicators of guinea pig health. Healthy guinea pigs show genuine excitement about meals, maintain consistent eating schedules, and demonstrate clear preferences for favorite foods while still eating balanced diets.

Active exploration and curiosity during natural activity periods shows guinea pigs who feel secure and energetic. Healthy guinea pigs investigate their environment, show interest in new sounds or activities, and move confidently around their habitat.

Normal social interactions with both guinea pig companions and human families indicate emotional and physical well-being. Healthy guinea pigs communicate normally through vocalizations and body language, share space comfortably with companions, and engage with their human families during daily care.

> **QUICK TIP**
> *Weigh your guinea pig once a week. Sudden weight loss can be an early sign of illness.*

Regular grooming behavior shows guinea pigs who feel well enough to maintain normal hygiene and social activities. Healthy guinea pigs spend time cleaning themselves and often engage in mutual grooming with their companions.

Daily Health Monitoring Made Easy

Quick morning check (30 seconds per guinea pig): Look for evidence of normal overnight activity like eaten food and fresh droppings, check that both guinea pigs seem alert when they hear you moving around, and make sure water levels went down overnight.

Evening interaction assessment during their active period: Watch for normal movement patterns and energy levels, observe social interactions between guinea pig companions, notice their response to your presence and voice, and check their enthusiasm for dinner time.

Weekly weight monitoring helps track overall health trends. Use a small digital scale to weigh each guinea pig weekly, recording results in a simple log. Gradual changes are usually normal, but sudden weight gains or losses may indicate developing problems.

Learning your guinea pigs' normal patterns helps you spot meaningful changes early. Every guinea pig has individual personality traits, activity preferences, and daily routines that become familiar over time.

9.2 Common Health Challenges and Early Recognition

Understanding health problems that guinea pigs sometimes face helps you spot issues early when they're easiest to treat. The good news? Most guinea pig health problems are preventable with excellent care, and early recognition usually leads to successful treatment.

Respiratory Problems

Upper respiratory infections are probably the most common health challenge guinea pigs face, but they're usually very treatable when caught early.

Early signs to watch for: Slight increase in breathing rate, occasional sneezing (especially if it doesn't stop quickly), minor clear discharge from nose, decreased activity or appetite, and changes in normal guinea pig vocalizations.

When to contact your vet immediately: Obvious breathing difficulty or mouth breathing, colored discharge from nose or eyes (yellow, green, or bloody), rattling or wheezing sounds during breathing, refusal to eat or drink, and extreme lethargy or inability to move normally.

Prevention strategies: Maintain good habitat ventilation without drafts, keep bedding clean and dust-free, avoid sudden temperature changes, provide adequate space to prevent stress, and quarantine new guinea pigs before introducing them to your pair.

Digestive Issues

GI stasis (when the digestive system slows or stops) is a serious condition that requires immediate veterinary attention, but it's often preventable with proper care.

Warning signs: Decreased or absent droppings production, small, hard, or unusually shaped droppings, reduced appetite or complete food refusal, lethargy and hunched posture, and grinding teeth (which indicates pain in guinea pigs).

Emergency action: Contact your veterinarian immediately if guinea pigs stop eating for more than 12 hours or stop producing droppings for 12+ hours. GI stasis can become life-threatening quickly but responds well to prompt treatment.

Prevention through good care: Provide unlimited high-quality hay for proper fiber, maintain consistent, appropriate diet without sudden changes, ensure constant access to fresh water, minimize stress through stable environment, and monitor daily for normal eating and elimination patterns.

Skin and Coat Problems

External parasites like mites can cause itching and hair loss but are very treatable with proper veterinary care.

Signs that suggest parasites: Intense scratching or biting at skin, hair loss in patches or all over, red, irritated, or scabby skin, restlessness and obvious discomfort, and sometimes tiny moving specks visible in fur.

Skin infections can cause patches of hair loss, scaling, or changes in skin appearance, and they usually respond well to appropriate treatment.

Prevention strategies: Maintain clean habitat conditions, quarantine new guinea pigs before introduction, use quality hay and bedding from reputable sources, and monitor guinea pigs regularly during grooming for any skin changes.

Dental Problems

Overgrown teeth can develop when guinea pigs don't have adequate opportunities for natural wear, but this is usually preventable.

Signs of dental issues: Difficulty eating or dropping food while trying to eat, drooling or persistent wetness around mouth, visible overgrowth of front teeth, weight loss despite seeming interested in food, and reluctance to eat hay or other hard foods.

Prevention through proper diet: Provide unlimited timothy hay for natural tooth wear, offer appropriate chew toys made from safe woods, feed proper pellets that require chewing, avoid soft diets unless medically necessary, and monitor eating behavior for early changes.

QUICK TIP
Watch your guinea pig's droppings. Changes in size or shape can be a sign they need a vet check.

Urinary Problems

Bladder issues can develop but are often related to diet and are usually manageable with proper care.

Signs to watch for: Straining to urinate or producing small amounts, blood in urine (pink or red coloration), frequent positioning as if to urinate, white, gritty deposits in urine, and signs of discomfort during urination.

Prevention strategies: Provide balanced diet without excessive calcium for adult guinea pigs, ensure constant access to fresh water, maintain clean habitat conditions, and monitor for any changes in normal elimination patterns.

9.3 Building a Great Veterinary Relationship

Finding and working with a qualified exotic pet veterinarian is one of the most important investments you'll make in your guinea pigs' long-term health and your family's peace of mind.

Finding the Right Veterinarian

Exotic pet experience matters! Look for veterinarians who specifically advertise small mammal or exotic pet services. Guinea pig medicine is quite different from dog and cat medicine, so specialized experience makes a huge difference in treatment success.

Questions to ask potential vets: "How many guinea pigs do you treat regularly?" "What are the most common conditions you see in guinea pigs?" "Do you perform guinea pig surgeries and dental procedures?" "What emergency coverage do you provide?"

Evaluating veterinary clinics: Look for clean, well-organized facilities with proper equipment for small animals, staff who seem knowledgeable about guinea pig care, reasonable costs and clear payment policies, and convenient location and hours for your family's needs.

Preparing for Veterinary Visits

Transport preparation: Use secure carriers large enough for guinea pig pairs (they're less stressed together), include familiar bedding and a small amount of hay for longer visits, and bring any medications or special items your vet has recommended.

Information to bring: Prepare lists of questions or concerns, bring records of recent eating, drinking, and activity patterns, note any behavioral or physical changes you've observed, and have information about diet, housing, and any recent changes ready to share.

Making visits less stressful: Schedule appointments during guinea pig active periods when possible, bring both guinea pigs even if only one needs examination (for emotional support), ask your vet to explain procedures and findings in terms your family can understand, and follow up with questions if anything isn't clear.

Understanding Treatment Options

Medication considerations: Guinea pigs require special dosing due to their size and metabolism. Ask your vet to demonstrate proper administration techniques, understand potential side effects, and learn how to monitor treatment response at home.

When surgery might be needed: Some conditions require surgical treatment, but guinea pigs can handle procedures well with experienced veterinarians. Discuss surgeon experience with guinea pigs, anesthetic protocols designed for small animals, and post-operative care requirements.

Cost planning: Understand typical costs for routine care vs. emergency treatments, investigate pet insurance options that cover exotic animals, and discuss payment plans or options if major treatments are needed.

9.4 Emergency Preparedness and Basic First Aid

Being prepared for guinea pig emergencies helps you respond calmly and effectively while arranging professional veterinary care. Most emergencies are rare, but preparation gives you confidence to handle unexpected situations.

Recognizing True Emergencies

Breathing emergencies always require immediate veterinary attention: obvious difficulty breathing, gasping or mouth breathing, blue-tinged gums or tongue, and choking or inability to breathe normally.

Severe trauma from accidents or injuries needs prompt professional care: visible injuries with bleeding, inability to move normally after falls or accidents, obvious fractures or severe limping, and any head injuries or loss of consciousness.

Digestive emergencies can become life-threatening quickly: complete refusal to eat for 12+ hours, no droppings production for

> ### Basic First Aid Principles
>
> **Stay calm and think clearly** during emergencies. Your guinea pigs will pick up on your stress, and panic can lead to poor decisions that make situations worse.
>
> **Ensure safety first** for both you and your guinea pigs. Remove immediate dangers, handle frightened guinea pigs carefully to avoid bites, and secure the area to prevent further injuries.
>
> **Provide gentle support** while arranging veterinary care. Keep injured guinea pigs warm using soft towels or body heat, handle minimally and only as necessary, and speak softly to provide comfort without overstimulation.
>
> **Never attempt major first aid** beyond keeping guinea pigs safe and comfortable. Guinea pig emergencies require professional expertise, and well-meaning home treatment can sometimes make problems worse.

12+ hours, severe bloating or obviously hard abdomen, and signs of severe pain like constant teeth grinding.

Neurological problems indicate serious issues: seizures or convulsions, loss of balance or coordination, head tilting or circling behavior, and extreme disorientation or unresponsiveness.

Emergency Supplies to Keep Ready

Basic emergency kit: Clean, soft towels for warmth and gentle restraint, secure carrier for transport to veterinary care, flashlight for examination during power outages or dim conditions, and emergency contact information that's easily accessible.

Important information to maintain: Primary veterinarian's contact information including after-hours numbers, directions to nearest emergency exotic pet clinic, your guinea pigs' normal weight and basic health information, and current medications or special dietary requirements.

9.5 Prevention: The Best Health Strategy

Prevention through excellent daily care is far more effective and less stressful than treating established illnesses. Most guinea pig health issues are preventable through knowledgeable, consistent care and attention to their unique needs.

Environmental Health Support

Excellent habitat conditions prevent many common problems. Maintain consistent cleaning schedules that prevent ammonia buildup and bacterial growth, provide proper ventilation without drafts that could cause respiratory issues, use appropriate bedding materials that don't cause irritation, and ensure adequate space to prevent stress-related health problems.

Temperature and humidity management supports immune function. Keep guinea pig areas between 65-75°F consistently, avoid rapid temperature changes that stress immune systems, provide adequate air circulation year-round, and protect from seasonal extremes that could cause health problems.

Stress reduction strengthens natural disease resistance. Maintain predictable daily routines that help guinea pigs feel secure, respect guinea pig social needs through proper companionship, provide adequate hiding places and environmental enrichment, and minimize household chaos that could overwhelm sensitive guinea pigs.

Nutritional Health Foundation

Excellent nutrition prevents many serious conditions including scurvy, dental problems, and digestive disorders. Provide unlimited high-quality timothy hay for proper fiber and dental health, measured portions of appropriate pellets for concentrated nutrition, daily fresh vegetables rich in Vitamin C for essential vitamins, and constant access to clean, fresh water.

Proper food safety prevents digestive problems and poisoning. Store guinea pig foods properly to maintain quality and prevent contamination, introduce new foods gradually to prevent digestive upset, avoid all known toxic foods completely, and maintain clean food and water containers.

Regular Monitoring and Professional Care

Consistent observation helps identify problems when they're most treatable. Conduct daily informal health checks during normal care routines, perform weekly more detailed assessments including weight monitoring, and track any changes in normal patterns or behaviors.

Preventive veterinary care provides professional health monitoring. Schedule routine checkups even when guinea pigs seem perfectly healthy, maintain relationships with qualified exotic pet veterinarians, and follow recommended health monitoring schedules throughout your guinea pigs' lives.

Early intervention when small problems are noticed improves treatment success and reduces costs. Don't wait for minor issues to become major emergencies, seek professional advice when you notice changes in normal patterns, and follow through completely with recommended treatments.

Building Lifelong Health Habits

Family health awareness creates sustainable care systems. Educate all family members about normal guinea pig health signs, assign appropriate health monitoring responsibilities to different family members, and create communication systems so health concerns don't get overlooked.

Record keeping helps track health patterns over time. Maintain simple logs of weight, eating patterns, and any health concerns, take photos of any skin or physical changes to show veterinarians, and keep records of veterinary visits and treatments.

Understanding guinea pig health and maintaining excellent preventive care provides the foundation for 6-8 years of wonderful companionship. The investment in proper nutrition, environmental management, and veterinary relationships pays dividends in healthier, happier guinea pigs who enrich your family's life for many years.

....

Coming up in Chapter 10: Learn to establish sustainable daily, weekly, and monthly care routines that maintain guinea pig health while fitting into your family's busy schedule and lifestyle.

Chapter 10:
Daily, Weekly, and Monthly Care

10.1 Creating Care Routines That Work for Your Family

Great guinea pig care doesn't have to take over your life or stress out your family! The secret is building simple, sustainable routines that become as natural as any other daily habit. When you establish good patterns from the beginning, caring for your guinea pig pair feels rewarding rather than overwhelming.

QUICK TIP
Keep your guinea pig's cage clean by spot-cleaning daily. A tidy home helps prevent sickness.

The best guinea pig families find that consistent routines actually save time and reduce stress for everyone—including the guinea pigs, who love predictable schedules and knowing what to expect each day.

Making Daily Care Enjoyable

Morning check-in (5-10 minutes): Your guinea pigs will probably be settling down for their morning rest when you wake up, but you can still learn a lot about their health and happiness without disturbing them.

Start by looking around their habitat for signs of a good night—did they eat their hay and pellets? Is there evidence they were active and social? You're being a detective, gathering clues that everything is normal and wonderful in guinea pig land.

Check their water levels and top off if needed. Guinea pigs go through water more quickly than you might expect, especially if they're eating lots of fresh vegetables. Add fresh hay if their supply is running low—guinea pigs should never be without hay!

Evening interaction time (15-25 minutes): This is when your guinea pigs truly come alive and show their amazing personalities! It's the perfect time for feeding, gentle bonding, and just enjoying these delightful animals.

Prepare and serve their daily fresh vegetable "salad" during this naturally active period. Your guinea pigs will probably start wheeking with excitement

as soon as they hear you preparing their dinner—it's one of the best sounds in guinea pig ownership!

Give their measured pellet portions if you're using scheduled feeding. Many guinea pigs have strong opinions about dinner timing and will remind you if you're running late!

Use this time for gentle interaction, whether that's lap time, floor time, or simply watching them explore and socialize with each other. Guinea pigs are much more entertaining and interactive during their natural active periods.

Do basic habitat tidying by removing any wilted vegetables from earlier, spot-cleaning any heavily soiled areas, and making sure everything looks comfortable for their active evening and nighttime hours.

Building Sustainable Family Routines

Involve everyone appropriately: Different family members can handle different aspects of guinea pig care based on their ages, schedules, and interests. One person might love preparing the daily vegetable salads, while another enjoys the evening social time.

Create backup plans: Life gets busy sometimes! Know which tasks are absolutely essential (fresh water, basic feeding, hay availability) versus enjoyable extras (extended floor time, habitat redecorating). Having a "simplified care day" plan prevents guilt and ensures guinea pigs stay healthy during hectic periods.

Celebrate the efficiency of pairs: Caring for bonded guinea pig pairs is often easier than caring for single pets because they entertain each other, follow similar schedules, and create their own social enrichment.

10.2 Weekly Deep Cleaning That Builds Bonds

Once a week, your guinea pigs' home needs a thorough refresh that keeps them healthy while giving you a chance to really connect with them and monitor their well-being. With good planning, weekly cleaning becomes a family activity that everyone can enjoy.

Getting Ready for Success

Gather everything first: Collect fresh bedding, cleaning supplies, treats for your guinea pigs, and any replacement toys or accessories before starting. Having everything prepared makes the job flow smoothly and reduces stress for both you and your guinea pigs.

Set up comfortable temporary housing: Your guinea pig pair needs a safe, cozy place to stay during cleaning. A large carrier with familiar bedding, a temporary exercise pen, or a backup habitat works perfectly. Include a favorite hideout and some hay to keep them comfortable while you work.

Make it a positive experience: Talk softly to your guinea pigs throughout the process, offer occasional treats, and let them know what's happening. Many guinea pigs learn to associate cleaning day with positive attention and extra treats!

The Weekly Refresh Process

Remove and evaluate old bedding: Take out all used bedding materials while observing any patterns—which areas seem to be preferred bathrooms? Are there spots that stay cleaner? This information helps you understand your guinea pigs' habits and preferences.

Clean and inspect everything: Wash all removable components with guinea pig-safe cleaners, including food bowls, water bottles, hideouts, and toys. While cleaning, check for wear and tear that might need attention or replacement.

Health monitoring opportunities: Use cleaning time for weekly weight checks. When you handle guinea pigs for weighing or moving them, notice any changes in their coat condition, body weight, or general demeanor.

Create a fresh environment: Add new bedding to appropriate depth, refill hay areas generously, arrange accessories to provide variety and interest, and maybe add a new cardboard box or simple enrichment item for exploration.

Making Weekly Cleaning Family-Friendly

Age-appropriate tasks: Younger children can help gather supplies and talk to guinea pigs during the process. Older kids can handle more complex tasks like cleaning accessories or arranging fresh bedding. Adults handle guinea pig moving and any heavy lifting.

Time management: Most families find weekly cleaning takes 30-45 minutes when everyone helps. Working together makes the time pass quickly while teaching children about responsibility and animal care.

Quality time bonus: Many families discover that cleaning day becomes special bonding time when guinea pigs get extra attention, new experiences, and the satisfaction of a fresh, clean home.

10.3 Monthly Check-Ins and Planning

Once a month, take a step back to look at the bigger picture of your guinea pigs' health, happiness, and your family's care routines. This broader perspective helps you spot gradual changes and plan for future needs.

Comprehensive Health and Happiness Review

Look for patterns and changes: Compare your guinea pigs' current behavior, appetite, activity levels, and social interactions to what you've observed over the past month. Gradual changes are often easier to spot when you examine longer time periods.

Physical condition assessment: Evaluate coat quality, body condition, nail length, and overall appearance. Are grooming needs being met adequately? Do any physical care routines need adjustment?

Social relationship monitoring: How are your guinea pig pairs getting along? Are they still bonded and comfortable with each other, or have you noticed any changes in their interactions that might need attention?

Environmental satisfaction: Observe how your guinea pigs use their habitat. Are there areas they consistently avoid or features they don't seem to enjoy? This information helps you make improvements that enhance their quality of life.

Planning and Preparation

Supply management: Review your inventory of hay, bedding, food, and other essentials. Plan purchases to keep adequate supplies on hand while taking advantage of bulk buying opportunities when your budget allows.

Seasonal adjustments: Consider upcoming weather changes and how they might affect your guinea pigs' comfort or your care routines. Do you need to prepare for temperature changes, holiday schedules, or seasonal supply availability?

Family schedule planning: Look ahead at your family's upcoming commitments. Are there busy periods when you'll need simplified care routines? Times when you might want to introduce new enrichment or activities?

Health care scheduling: Plan any routine veterinary appointments, nail trimming sessions, or grooming needs that might be due in the coming month.

Equipment and Environment Assessment

Habitat evaluation: Assess whether your guinea pigs' housing continues to meet their needs effectively. Are they using all areas of their home? Do any components need repair, replacement, or upgrading?

Enrichment effectiveness: Which toys, activities, or environmental features do your guinea pigs enjoy most? What could you add, change, or rotate to keep their environment interesting and engaging?

Family routine evaluation: Are your current care routines working well for everyone? Do any aspects need adjustment to better fit changing family schedules or guinea pig needs?

10.4 Seasonal Care That Keeps Guinea Pigs Comfortable

Different seasons bring unique opportunities and challenges for guinea pig care. Understanding and preparing for these changes helps you keep your guinea pigs comfortable and healthy year-round.

Spring and Summer Considerations

Increased activity and energy: Many guinea pigs become more active and social as daylight hours increase and temperatures warm up. You might notice more popcorning, increased appetite, or greater interest in floor time and exploration.

Temperature management: During warmer weather, provide cooling options like ceramic tiles for guinea pigs to rest on, ensure excellent ventilation around their habitat, monitor for signs of overheating (panting, lethargy, reduced appetite), and make sure fresh, cool water is always available.

Fresh food opportunities: Take advantage of seasonal vegetables when they're at peak quality and reasonable prices. Spring and summer often provide wonderful variety for daily guinea pig salads with local, fresh options.

Outdoor time possibilities: If your family chooses to provide supervised outdoor time, warm weather offers more opportunities. Always ensure secure enclosures, predator protection, shade availability, and constant supervision during any outdoor adventures.

Fall and Winter Adjustments

Comfort and warmth: Monitor habitat temperatures as outdoor weather cools. Provide extra bedding for comfort, ensure good ventilation without drafts, and consider safe supplemental heating if your home gets quite cold.

Supply planning and storage: Stock up on hay, bedding, and other essentials before winter weather makes shopping more challenging. Plan storage to keep supplies dry and fresh throughout colder months.

Holiday and family schedule management: Busy holiday periods require advance planning to ensure guinea pig care remains consistent. Arrange pet care for travel well in advance, and prepare simplified care routines for hectic times.

Indoor air quality: Winter often means closed houses with less natural air circulation. Ensure guinea pig habitats maintain adequate ventilation while avoiding cold drafts that could cause health problems.

> **QUICK TIP**
> *Set a regular time for feeding and play. Guinea pigs feel safer and happier with a steady routine.*

Year-Round Routine Consistency

Maintaining stability: While seasonal adjustments help keep guinea pigs comfortable, the foundation of excellent care remains consistent throughout the year. Regular feeding, cleaning, and interaction schedules help guinea pigs feel secure regardless of external changes.

Flexible planning: Build care routines that can adapt to seasonal changes and family schedule variations while maintaining the essential elements that keep guinea pigs healthy and happy.

Health vigilance: Some health challenges are more common during specific seasons, but good observation, preventive care, and responsive adjustments remain important throughout the entire year.

Creating and maintaining excellent care routines provides the foundation for your guinea pigs' long-term health and happiness while fitting realistically into your family's lifestyle. These routines become easier and more automatic over time, creating sustainable patterns that benefit both guinea pigs and families for years to come.

•••••••••••••••••••••••••••••••••••••

Coming up in Chapter 11: Learn to identify and solve common challenges that arise during guinea pig ownership, from behavioral issues to family schedule changes, and discover when to seek professional help for the best outcomes.

Chapter 11: When Challenges Arise

11.1 Challenges Are Normal (And Usually Solvable!)

Here's something every experienced guinea pig family knows: even the best-cared-for guinea pigs sometimes present challenges that puzzle, surprise, or worry their families. The great news? Most guinea pig challenges have straightforward explanations and solutions once you understand what your pets are trying to communicate.

Think of challenges as your guinea pigs' way of telling you they need something adjusted, improved, or understood differently. Rather than meaning you're doing something wrong, most challenges are opportunities to become an even better guinea pig family!

Understanding Guinea Pig Communication Through Behavior

Guinea pigs are excellent communicators who use behavior to tell you about their needs, preferences, and comfort levels. When behavior changes or seems problematic, they're usually trying to share important information about their environment, health, or social situation.

The detective mindset helps: Approach guinea pig challenges with curiosity rather than frustration. What might your guinea pigs be trying to tell you? What environmental factors could be influencing their behavior? This perspective often leads to quick solutions that benefit everyone.

Most challenges fall into predictable categories: social dynamics between guinea pig pairs, environmental factors that cause stress or discomfort, health issues that affect behavior, and family circumstances that require care adjustments. Understanding these categories helps you identify solutions more quickly.

11.2 Social Dynamics and Pair Relationships

Guinea pig pairs naturally develop complex social relationships that sometimes need gentle management or environmental adjustments to maintain harmony.

Understanding Normal vs. Concerning Social Behavior

Normal pair dynamics include brief dominance displays where one guinea pig establishes leadership, gentle competition over favorite foods or prime

real estate, occasional mild disagreements that resolve quickly, and clear social hierarchies that both guinea pigs accept comfortably.

Signs that intervention might help include persistent chasing that doesn't end peacefully, one guinea pig preventing another from accessing food, water, or shelter, visible stress in either guinea pig (weight loss, excessive hiding, reduced activity), and escalating conflicts rather than stable social arrangements.

Most social issues respond well to environmental changes: providing more space if guinea pigs seem crowded, adding extra resources so there's less competition, creating separate territories within shared habitats, and ensuring both guinea pigs have escape routes and private spaces when needed.

When Guinea Pig Relationships Need Support

Resource competition often underlies social tensions. The solution? **More of everything!** Provide multiple food bowls, water sources, and hideouts so guinea pigs don't need to compete for essentials. Strategic placement of resources around the habitat prevents bottlenecks and reduces stress.

Personality conflicts sometimes develop, especially during adolescence or when guinea pigs are adjusting to new living situations. **Environmental enrichment** often helps by giving guinea pigs more interesting things to focus on besides each other, providing opportunities for individual activities within shared space, and reducing boredom that can lead to social tensions.

QUICK TIP
Separate guinea pigs if fights break out. Give them space and reintroduce slowly in a larger cage.

Temporary separations might be needed if guinea pigs seem stressed or overwhelmed by social dynamics. This doesn't mean failure—sometimes guinea pigs need a brief break to reset their relationship, especially during illness, environmental changes, or hormonal fluctuations.

Supporting Healthy Pair Relationships

Adequate space prevents many social problems by allowing guinea pigs to establish individual territories while maintaining their social bond.

Environmental complexity provides multiple interesting areas, hiding spots, and activity centers that give guinea pigs options for togetherness or individual space.

Consistent routines help guinea pig pairs feel secure and cooperative.

Monitoring without overreacting allows you to distinguish between normal social adjustment and situations that need intervention.

11.3 Environmental Solutions That Work

Many guinea pig challenges stem from environmental factors that are easily adjustable once you identify them. The good news? Environmental solutions often improve life for both guinea pigs and families!

Common Environmental Challenges

Temperature and comfort issues can affect guinea pig behavior and health.

Summer solutions include providing cooling options like ceramic tiles, ensuring excellent ventilation, monitoring for overheating signs, and adjusting habitat location away from heat sources.

Winter considerations involve preventing drafts while maintaining fresh air, providing extra bedding for comfort, monitoring for adequate warmth, and ensuring guinea pigs stay active and social during indoor seasons.

Noise and household activity sometimes overwhelm sensitive guinea pigs. **Creating calm zones** helps by choosing quieter habitat locations when possible, using soft furnishings to absorb household sounds, maintaining predictable household routines, and providing secure hiding options for overstimulated guinea pigs.

Odor and Cleanliness Management

Persistent odor issues usually indicate problems that are solvable with adjustments to cleaning routines, ventilation, or health care.

Practical solutions include: increasing cleaning frequency if current routines aren't adequate, improving air circulation around guinea pig areas, evaluating bedding choices for better odor control, spot-cleaning high-use areas more frequently, and checking for health issues that might contribute to unusual odors.

Working with guinea pig natural behaviors: Understanding where guinea pigs prefer to eliminate helps you place litter areas strategically, provide appropriate bathroom facilities, and maintain cleanliness without fighting natural preferences.

Space and Enrichment Adjustments

Signs guinea pigs need more stimulation: repetitive behaviors like bar chewing or pacing, decreased interest in normal activities, social tensions that seem related to boredom, and general restlessness or dissatisfaction with their environment.

Enrichment solutions that work: rotating toys and accessories weekly to maintain novelty, creating foraging opportunities through scattered feeding, providing climbing structures and varied textures, and offering safe exploration opportunities during supervised floor time.

Space optimization includes using vertical space effectively, creating multiple activity centers, providing clear pathways between resources, and ensuring guinea pigs can engage in natural behaviors comfortably.

11.4 Family Dynamics and Schedule Changes

Family circumstances naturally change over time, and successful guinea pig ownership means adapting care routines to work with evolving family situations while maintaining excellent pet welfare.

Managing Changing Responsibilities

When children's interests fluctuate (which is completely normal!), successful families have backup plans that ensure guinea pig welfare without creating guilt or conflict.

Sustainable solutions include: distributing care responsibilities among multiple family members, creating simple routines that become automatic habits, maintaining adult oversight regardless of children's involvement levels, and celebrating guinea pig care successes to keep motivation positive.

Building life skills through pet care: Assign age-appropriate responsibilities that grow with children's abilities, provide support and guidance without taking over completely, recognize that learning involves mistakes and adjustments, and emphasize how guinea pig care builds character and responsibility.

Adapting to Schedule Changes

Family schedule shifts from work changes, school transitions, or life circumstances require thoughtful adaptation rather than stress.

Practical strategies: develop flexible care routines that work with various schedules, train multiple family members in essential guinea pig care, create simplified care plans for particularly busy periods, and maintain guinea pig routine stability even when family schedules change.

Communication and planning help ensure guinea pig care doesn't fall through cracks during transitions.

Family meetings about pet responsibilities, **clear backup plans** for emergencies or schedule conflicts, and **realistic expectations** about what different family members can handle create sustainable systems.

Managing Life Transitions

Moving with guinea pigs requires planning but is completely manageable with preparation. Transport guinea pigs safely in secure carriers with familiar bedding, set up their habitat immediately in the new location, maintain familiar routines to provide security during transition, and monitor for stress signs while providing extra attention and comfort.

Financial adjustments sometimes require creative solutions for maintaining excellent guinea pig care. Focus on essentials first (food, basic veterinary care, adequate housing), explore cost-saving strategies like bulk buying and DIY enrichment, connect with guinea pig communities for resource sharing and support, and prioritize preventive care to avoid expensive emergency treatments.

11.5 Health-Related Behavior Changes

Sometimes guinea pig behavior changes indicate developing health issues that need attention. Learning to recognize these patterns helps ensure prompt, appropriate care.

Recognizing Health-Related Behavior Changes

Decreased appetite or eating changes often indicate health issues requiring veterinary attention. **Social withdrawal** from guinea pig companions or human families can signal discomfort or illness. **Activity level changes** like decreased movement or unusual restlessness might suggest developing problems.

QUICK TIP

If your guinea pig suddenly stops eating or drinking, contact a vet right away. Quick action can save their life.

Pain indicators include reluctance to move normally, changes in posture or positioning, unusual vocalizations during normal activities, and decreased grooming or social behaviors.

When behavior changes suggest health concerns: contact your veterinarian promptly rather than waiting to see if problems resolve independently, provide detailed information about observed changes, and maintain normal care routines while seeking professional guidance.

Supporting Guinea Pigs During Health Challenges

Environmental modifications can help guinea pigs feel more comfortable during illness or recovery. **Easier access** to food and water, **softer bedding** for comfort, **quieter environments** to reduce stress, and **maintaining social companionship** when medically appropriate all support healing.

Family support during health challenges includes following veterinary instructions carefully, monitoring for improvement or concerns, providing emotional comfort through gentle attention, and maintaining hope and positive attitudes that guinea pigs often sense and respond to.

11.6 Knowing When to Seek Help

Recognizing when challenges exceed your family's ability to solve them independently ensures guinea pigs get appropriate professional help while preventing minor issues from becoming serious problems.

Professional Resources for Guinea Pig Challenges

Veterinary consultation helps with health-related behavior changes, persistent problems that don't respond to environmental adjustments, questions about normal vs. concerning guinea pig behavior, and guidance for complex care situations.

Guinea pig communities provide valuable support through experienced owner advice, resource sharing and practical tips, emotional support during challenging periods, and connections to local professionals and services.

Professional services like experienced guinea pig groomers, pet sitters with small animal experience, and behavioral consultants familiar with guinea pig needs can provide specialized help when needed.

Making Decisions in Guinea Pigs' Best Interests

Quality of life considerations sometimes require difficult decisions about care arrangements, living situations, or treatment options. **Focus on guinea pig welfare** rather than family attachment or guilt when evaluating challenging situations.

When rehoming might be necessary: severe allergies that don't respond to management, major life changes that prevent adequate care, persistent welfare issues that can't be resolved, or family circumstances that make continued care impossible.

Responsible rehoming involves finding appropriate new homes through guinea pig rescues or experienced families, providing complete health and care information, and ensuring new families understand guinea pig social needs and long-term commitments.

Building Problem-Solving Skills

Every challenge teaches valuable lessons about guinea pig behavior, family dynamics, and creative problem-solving that make you better caregivers for current and future pets.

Developing confidence through successfully managing guinea pig challenges builds skills that transfer to other areas of life and creates stronger family bonds through shared problem-solving experiences.

Community contribution happens when experienced families share their knowledge and support newcomers facing similar challenges, creating positive cycles that benefit guinea pig welfare everywhere.

Most challenges in guinea pig ownership are temporary and solvable with patience, creativity, and appropriate support. The key is approaching problems as normal parts of pet ownership while maintaining perspective about what's truly concerning versus what's simply part of learning to live together successfully.

....

Coming up in Chapter 12: Learn about your guinea pigs' life journey from young adults through their senior years, and discover how to make the most of every stage while planning for the future with wisdom and love.

Chapter 12: Growing Together

12.1 Your Guinea Pig's Life Journey

Understanding your guinea pigs' journey through different life stages helps you provide the best care while preparing emotionally for the natural changes that come with their 6-8 year lifespans. Each stage brings its own joys and challenges.

Baby and Young Guinea Pig Stage (0-6 months)

Amazing growth happens fast: Baby guinea pigs change from tiny, vulnerable creatures to active, curious young adults in just a few months. If you adopted very young guinea pigs, you've been amazed by how quickly they developed new skills and distinct personalities.

Extra nutritional needs: Growing guinea pigs need more protein and unlimited food access because their small size makes them vulnerable to going without food for too long.

Prime socialization time: Gentle, consistent interaction during these early months helps develop confident, well-adjusted adult guinea pigs who are comfortable with human families. This is when your guinea pigs learned whether humans are friends or threats.

Building pair bonds: Young guinea pigs adopted together typically form the strongest lifelong relationships during this period, creating the social foundation that will last their entire lives.

Adult Prime Years (6 months-4 years)

Peak performance time: This is when guinea pigs are at their healthiest, most active, and most interactive. Many families find this the most rewarding period of guinea pig ownership because their pets' personalities really shine through.

Personality becomes clear: During adult years, your guinea pigs' individual traits and preferences become obvious. Some are natural athletes who love floor time, others are architects who constantly rearrange their bedding, and many are little comedians with unique quirks that make you laugh.

Building your relationship: The bonds formed during this period often provide the most emotional rewards of guinea pig ownership. Your guinea pigs learned to recognize your voice, wheek when you appear, and develop trust in your daily care.

Senior Years (4+ years)

Gradual changes begin: Your guinea pigs might start moving a bit slower, sleeping more, or showing minor changes in appetite. These changes often happen so slowly they're barely noticeable at first.

FUN FACT
Senior guinea pigs often become more cuddly and social.

Comfort becomes priority: Senior guinea pigs may need softer bedding, easier access to food and water, or modified habitat arrangements. Simple adjustments can maintain their quality of life significantly.

Deeper bonds often develop: Many senior guinea pigs become more affectionate and content to spend quiet time with their families. These gentle interactions can be deeply meaningful for both pets and families.

12.2 Expanding Your Knowledge and Community

Growing as a guinea pig owner means continuing to learn and connecting with other people who share your interest in these amazing animals.

Continuing Your Education

Advanced topics: As you gain experience, you might want to learn about specialized guinea pig nutrition, advanced environmental enrichment, or deeper understanding of guinea pig behavior and social dynamics.

Stay current: Guinea pig care continues to evolve as researchers learn more about what these animals need to thrive. Following reputable sources helps you stay updated on best practices.

Document your journey: Keeping track of what you learn helps you remember important information and creates valuable knowledge to share with others starting their guinea pig adventures.

Joining the Guinea Pig Community

Local connections: Finding other guinea pig enthusiasts in your area provides face-to-face support, opportunities to see different care approaches, and friendships based on shared interests in excellent animal care.

Online communities: Quality guinea pig groups offer broader perspectives, access to experts worldwide, and support available whenever you need help or want to share experiences.

Share your knowledge: As you gain experience, helping newcomers and mentoring new owners builds stronger communities while reinforcing your own understanding of good guinea

12.3 When It's Time to Say Goodbye

Planning for your guinea pigs' end-of-life care is one of the hardest parts of pet ownership. However, thinking about these issues ahead of time helps ensure final decisions reflect love and your guinea pigs' best interests.

Recognizing Quality of Life Changes

QUICK TIP
Prepare for goodbye with kindness. When a guinea pig reaches the end of its life, gentle care and comfort are the best gifts you can give.

Physical comfort signs: Watch for changes in your guinea pigs' ability to move around comfortably, eat and drink normally, or perform basic grooming. Difficulty with these essential activities can indicate declining quality of life.

Behavioral changes: Loss of interest in normal activities, withdrawal from guinea pig companions, disrupted daily patterns, or inability to perform natural behaviors like exploring may signal declining comfort.

Social considerations: Changes in relationships with guinea pig companions—either becoming overly clingy or withdrawing completely—can indicate health or comfort issues requiring attention.

Making Compassionate Decisions

Veterinary guidance helps families understand what guinea pigs are experiencing and what options exist for maintaining comfort and dignity. Experienced exotic pet veterinarians can provide objective assessment and support during difficult decision-making periods.

Family discussions should include everyone who has been involved in guinea pig care, with age-appropriate participation for children who need support and understanding during this difficult time.

Quality vs. quantity: Sometimes the most loving decision involves preventing suffering rather than extending life as long as possible. Focus on your guinea pigs' comfort and dignity rather than simply buying more time.

Supporting Surviving Guinea Pigs

When one guinea pig in a bonded pair dies, the survivor often grieves and may need extra attention, comfort, and possibly new companionship to maintain their social needs and emotional health.

Some guinea pigs benefit from being present during peaceful euthanasia, while others do better with gradual separation. Your veterinarian can help you decide what's most appropriate for your specific situation.

Introducing new companions to surviving guinea pigs requires careful consideration of timing, compatibility, and the emotional readiness of both surviving guinea pigs and family members.

Honoring Your Guinea Pigs' Memory

Celebrating your relationship: Focus on the joy, learning, and love your guinea pigs brought to your family throughout their lives. Create photo collections, memory books, or simple ceremonies that honor their impact on your family's life and development.

Understanding grief: Losing beloved pets creates real sadness that deserves recognition and support. Children especially need help understanding that grief over pet loss is normal and shows the depth of love and connection you shared.

Creating positive legacies: Consider donations to guinea pig rescue organizations, sharing your knowledge with other families, or volunteering to help other guinea pigs in need. These actions create positive outcomes from your loss while honoring your pets' memory.

12.4 Considering Your Next Guinea Pig

Deciding whether and when to welcome additional guinea pigs requires careful consideration of emotional readiness, practical circumstances, and lessons learned from your experience.

Timing Your Decision

Emotional readiness varies: Family members process grief differently and may feel ready for new relationships at different times. Some people benefit from new companionship quickly, while others need extended time to heal.

Surviving guinea pig needs: If you lose one guinea pig from a bonded pair, the survivor typically needs a new companion for their social and emotional health. However, introductions should be planned carefully.

Family agreement matters: Decisions about new pets should reflect everyone's feelings rather than pressure from some family members. Children especially need their emotions respected during these decisions.

Learning integration: Consider what worked well with your previous guinea pigs, what you might change, and how your knowledge and skills have developed. This experience makes you better caregivers for future pets.

Applying Your Experience

Improved care opportunities: Your experience creates confidence and knowledge that benefits new guinea pigs significantly. You understand guinea pig needs, can recognize health issues earlier, and know how to create enriching environments.

Realistic expectations: Previous experience helps you understand individual guinea pig personalities, social dynamics, and bonding processes. This knowledge prevents disappointment while helping you appreciate each guinea pig's unique qualities.

12.5 Your Guinea Pig Journey Continues

Your experience with guinea pigs represents more than just caring for small pets. It's an opportunity to develop compassion, responsibility, and appreciation for animals while creating cherished family memories.

The skills you develop, relationships you build, and knowledge you gain through guinea pig ownership often influence other areas of life, creating positive effects that extend far beyond pet care. Whether you choose to welcome one pair of guinea pigs or many throughout your life, each relationship offers unique rewards and learning opportunities.

Great guinea pig ownership combines scientific knowledge with compassionate care, creating experiences that teach responsibility while providing years of joy and companionship. You now have the tools and understanding to provide exceptional care throughout guinea pigs' entire 6-8 year lifespans while building meaningful relationships that benefit both your family and your pets.

Remember that every guinea pig deserves a family that approaches their care with knowledge, patience, and love. By reading this book and taking guinea pig ownership seriously, you're already demonstrating the kind of thoughtful, responsible approach that leads to wonderful experiences for both pets and families.

Quick Reference & Emergency Guide

Emergency Contacts (Fill In!)

Primary Exotic Vet: _____ **Phone:** _____
Emergency Vet: _____ **Phone:** _____
Backup Caregiver: _____ **Phone:** _____
Poison Control: _____ **Phone:** _____

Call Vet IMMEDIATELY If:

- **Breathing:** Difficulty breathing, wheezing, mouth breathing, gasping

- **Digestive:** No eating for 12+ hours, no droppings for 12+ hours, severe bloating

- **Injury:** Bleeding, obvious injury, inability to move normally

- **Neurological:** Seizures, loss of balance, head tilt, unresponsive

- **Other:** Extreme lethargy, discharge from eyes/nose, signs of pain (teeth grinding)

Basic First Aid (Get Vet Care Too!)

- **Minor cuts:** Clean gently, apply light pressure, keep warm, transport to vet

- **Overheating:** Move to cool area, offer water, apply cool (not cold) cloths, call vet

- **Choking:** Check mouth gently for visible objects, never force removal, go to vet immediately

- **Poisoning:** Remove from source, save sample of poison, DON'T induce vomiting, rush to vet

Normal vs. Concerning Behavior

NORMAL (Don't Panic)	CONCERNING (Monitor)	URGENT (Call Vet)
Active evenings/mornings	Eating/drinking less	No appetite 12+ hours
Wheeking for food	Hiding more than usual	No droppings 12+ hours
Popcorning when excited	Minor lethargy	Difficulty breathing
Brief dominance displays	Small changes in routine	Obvious pain/distress
Sleeping during day	Occasional soft stool	Bleeding or injury
Eating hay constantly	Less social interaction	Seizures or collapse

Quick Daily Health Check (30 seconds)

- **Eyes:** Clear and bright?
- **Breathing:** Quiet and regular?
- **Movement:** Walking normally?
- **Appetite:** Evidence of eating hay/pellets?
- **Elimination:** Normal droppings present?
- **Social:** Interacting normally with companion?

Emergency Kit Essentials

- Small towels and carrier
- Digital scale
- Small syringe
- Styptic powder
- Flashlight
- This guide
- Vet contact information

Key Reminders

☑ **DO:** Stay calm, handle gently, take notes, trust your instincts

✗ **DON'T:** Give human meds, force food/water, wait with serious symptoms

Remember: You know your guinea pig best. If something seems off, call your vet!

INDEX

A
Abyssinian guinea pigs, 14
activity levels, 95
adjustment period, 48–50
adult guinea pigs, 44–45, 62, 124
age considerations, 44–45
aggression, 31
American guinea pigs, 12–13
apples, 69
attention-seeking behaviors, 57
avocado, 69, 74

B
baby guinea pigs, 44, 62, 75, 123–124
bananas, 70
beans, 74
bedding, 37–38
beets, 68
behavioral challenges, 113–116, 119–120
bell peppers, 64, 66–67
berries, 68
body language, 30, 51–53
bonded pairs, 22, 24–25, 54–55, 124, 128. See also pairs
breathing problems, 100
breeders, 46
breeds, 12–15
broccoli, 64, 67
brushing, 85–87

C
C&C cages, 35–36
cages, 35–37. See also habitats
care routines, 105–112, 117–118
chattering, 54
cherry tomatoes, 68
chocolate, 74
climate, 39–40
coats, 94, 97
commercial cages, 36
communication

body language, 30, 51–53
with humans, 56–58
pain and illness cues, 52–53
sounds, 53–54
stress and fear signals, 52
understanding guinea pig, 113–114
cruciferous vegetables, 64, 67

D
daily care routines, 105–107
daily checks, 91
daily health monitoring, 95, 131
daily life, 54–56
daily schedule, 15
dairy products, 73
dangerous foods, 73–75
dehydration, 73
dental health, 90–91
dental problems, 97–98
diet, 59–61
digestive issues, 96–97, 100–101
digestive problems, 73

E
ear care, 89
eating, 54, 94, 119
elderly guinea pigs, 30
emergency preparedness, 100–101
emergency response, to poisoning, 75
emergency supplies, 101, 131
end-of-life issues, 126–128
enrichment, 40, 81, 83, 115, 117
environmental challenges, 116–117
equipment assessment, 110
essential items checklist, 41
evening check-ins, 106
exercise, 24, 40, 80–81
exploration, 95
eyes, 93

F

fall care, 111–112
family dynamics, 117–118
family readiness assessment, 19–20
family routines, 107, 110
fear signals, 52
female pairs, 26
financial costs, 17, 32–33
first aid, 101, 130
first day, 48–50
fleece bedding, 37–38
flooring, 37–38
"floor space," 35
floor time, 80–81
food
    dangerous, 73–75
    fresh, 64–70
    hay, 60, 61–63
    human, 74
    pellets, 70–71
    toxic, 69, 74
food containers, 39
food safety, 103
food sharing, 57
foraging games, 83
fresh foods, 64–70
fruits, 68–70

G
garlic, 74
GI statis, 96–97
grapes, 69
grazing, 54, 59, 60
grief, 128–129
grooming, 24, 54–55, 84–89, 95
    brushing, 85–87
    ear care, 89
    nail trimming, 87–89
    professional, 91–92
growth monitoring, 75
guinea pig community, 125–126
guinea pigs
    bodies of, 77–78
    breeds, 12–15
    choosing, 43–45
    introduction to, 10–11
    safe handling, 77–79
    social needs of, 21–23
    sources for, 45–47
    training, 82–83

H
habitats
    assessment of, 110
    budget-friendly, 40–42
    DIY solutions, 40
    essential features for, 37–39
    health and, 102
    options for, 35–37
    outdoor housing, 36–37
    for pairs, 32–33
    setup costs, 17, 32
    space requirements, 16–17, 34–35
    temperature and climate for, 39–40
    weekly cleaning, 107–109
hairless guinea pigs, 15
handling
    lap time, 79–80
    safe, 77–79
    two-handed approach to, 78
hay, 60, 61–63
hay management, 39
health indicators, 43–44, 93–94, 119
health monitoring, 95, 103, 108
health problems, 96–98
    behavior changes due to, 119–120
    dental problems, 97–98
    digestive issues, 96–97, 100–101
    emergency preparedness, 100–101
    neurological problems, 101
    prevention of, 102–104
    respiratory problems, 96
    skin and coat issues, 97
    urinary problems, 98
herbs, 66, 68
hideouts, 38–39, 41, 81, 83
houseplants, 74

human foods, 74
hydration, 72–73

I
iceberg lettuce, 66
illness, 30
illness cues, 52–53
introduction techniques, 28–30

L
lap time, 79–80
leafy greens, 64, 66, 67
learning styles, 82–83
lettuce, 66
lifespan, 17, 19
life stages, 123–125
life transitions, 119
long-haired guinea pigs, 13–14, 46, 85–86

M
male pairs, 26–27
meal timing, 71
medications, 99–100
melon, 69
mental stimulation, 40
money-saving strategies, 40–41
monthly check-ins, 109–110
morning check-ins, 105–106
mutual grooming, 54–55

N
nail trimming, 87–89
name recognition, 82
natural behaviors, 54–56
neurological problems, 101
noise, 116
noses, 94
nutrition, 59–76, 102–103
    fresh vegetables, 64–68
    hay, 60, 61–63
    pellets, 70–71
    pregnant or nursing guinea pigs, 62, 76
    senior guinea pigs, 76

    special dietary considerations, 75–76
    vitamin C, 60, 63–65
    water, 72–73
    young guinea pigs, 62, 75

O
odor issues, 116–117
onions, 74
oranges, 69
outdoor housing, 36–37

P
pain cues, 52–53
pain indicators, 119
pairs
    age considerations for, 27
    to avoid, 28
    benefits of, 22, 24–25, 33
    choosing compatible, 26–28
    introduction techniques, 28–30
    personality matching, 27
    same-sex, 26–27
    social behaviors of, 54–55
    social dynamics of, 114–116
    space planning for, 32–33
parasites, 97
pears, 69
pellets, 70–71
personality, 11–12, 15, 27, 81, 115, 124
Peruvian guinea pigs, 13
pet carriers, 47
pet stores, 46–47
plants, toxic, 74–75
poisoning, 75
popcorning, 10, 54
potatoes, 74
pregnant or nursing guinea pigs, 62, 76
processed foods, 73
professional groomers, 91–92
purring, 53–54
puzzle feeding, 83

Q

quarantine, 28

R
readiness checklist, 18
red flags, 44, 50
rehoming, 121
rescue organizations, 45–46
resource competition, 115
respiratory problems, 96
Rex guinea pigs, 14
rhubarb, 69, 74
Romaine lettuce, 66
root vegetables, 67–68
routines, developing, 48–49

S
schedule changes, 117–118
screaming, 54
scurvy, 63–64
seasonal care, 111–112
senior guinea pigs, 45, 76, 124–125
Sheltie guinea pigs, 13
shopping tips, 40–42
short-haired breeds, 12–13, 85
Silkie guinea pigs, 13
single guinea pigs, 23, 24–25, 30–32
skinny pigs, 15
skin problems, 97
social behaviors, 54–55, 114–116
social dynamics, 21–23, 114–116
social grooming, 24
social interactions, 95
social nature, 6, 10, 78–79
sounds, 53–54, 57
space requirements, 16–17, 34–35
special dietary considerations, 75–76
spinach, 74
spring care, 111
squealing, 54
starter setup, 41
stress reduction, 102
stress signals, 52
summer care, 111, 116

surgery, 100
sweet potatoes, 67–68

T
target training, 82
teeth, 61, 71, 90–91, 97–98
teeth chattering, 54
temperature, 39–40, 102, 116
time commitment, 15–16, 33
timothy hay, 61–63
toxic foods, 69, 74
toxic plants, 74–75
toy rotation, 40
training, 82–83
transition periods, 31
transporting home, 47–48
trauma, 100
travel tips, 47–48
trust building, 48–50, 52, 78–79

U
upper respiratory infections, 96
urinary problems, 74, 98

V
vegetables, 64–68
veterinary care, 98–100, 103, 120
    for grooming, 92
vitamin C, 60, 63–65

W
water, 72–73
weekly cleaning, 107–109
weekly schedule, 16
weight monitoring, 95
wheeking, 10, 53, 56
winter care, 111–112, 116

Y
young guinea pigs, 62, 75, 123–124

www.ingramcontent.com/pod-product-compliance
Lightning Source LLC
Chambersburg PA
CBHW082209070526
44585CB00020B/2349